Manners from Heaven

Manners from Heaven

The easier way to better behaviour for all the family

Sean Davoren

with Sue Carr

ORION

First published in trade paperback in Great Britain in 2005 by
Orion Books
an imprint of the Orion Publishing Group Ltd
Orion House, 5 Upper St Martin's Lane,
London WC2H 9EA

10 9 8 7 6 5 4 3 2 1

A CIP catalogue record for this book is
available from the British Library.

ISBN: 0 75287 213 3

Illustrations: Emily Faccini

Printed in Great Britain by
Clays Ltd, St Ives plc

Every effort has been made to fulfil requirements with regard to reproducing copyright material. The author and publisher will be glad to rectify any omissions at the earliest opportunity.

www.orionbooks.co.uk

Contents

From Sean: To my father and mother. Thank you for my good start in life! And love to my wife and my children. Thank you for putting up with me!

From Sue: To my mother, father and stepfather, who despaired of me ever becoming a – vaguely – well-mannered grown-up! And to all my friends who tirelessly try to give their children the best possible start in life.

Acknowledgements

From Sean:

I'd like to thank Jess for encouraging me to write this book and also thank you, Ian, and everyone at Orion for helping us make this book the best it could be.

Thank you, Emily, for all the wonderful illustrations, Terry and Giuliana for the great photos, and Christian for the Scorcese-inspired filmwork for the research groups.

Thank you to everyone at the Lanesborough for your continued support of my classes and this book.

And Sue for all the fun and laughs during our time together and the friendship.

From Sue:

A big thank you to all the parents and children who gave us their precious time to run through each chapter so we could see that the chapters actually worked. This book wouldn't be the book it is without you.

Special thanks to Sean for being such a wonderfully open, easy person to interview. You're up there with Sean Connery!

Thank you Lucas and Will for all your hugs and kisses when I was fed up with editing and last but certainly not least, Piers, thank you for being there, always.

Manners
from Heaven

Foreword

I first met Sean at one of his etiquette classes for children. I was there to see whether he was as good as people said he was, and to see whether his classes would translate into a book.

To be honest, I couldn't quite get my head around how anyone could make the subject of good manners inspiring – especially to children aged between six and twelve years old. I looked down the list of topics he was going to cover: laying the table, writing thank-you letters, why a soup and dessert spoon are different shapes … It didn't sound like a lot of fun. But the class was a real eye-opener. The two hours went quickly, the children loved all the games Sean had devised and, at the end when they did a quiz, they all put their hands up to answer his questions. The children were not only keen, interested and anything but bored, but they'd obviously taken in everything Sean had said.

Sean is from Limerick, and, like Terry Wogan, he has an easy banter and a sense of fun that's instantly infectious. His greatest talent is that he can make children laugh and want to learn at the same time. And – dare I say it – I think he even manages to stir in some children their first feelings of empathy…

SEAN: Do you all like going to parties?

ALL: Yes!!!

SEAN: What do you like about them?

LITTLE BOY: Food fights!

SEAN: Do you indeed?

ALL: YES! Food fights! Cream cakes – splat on your head! On the wall! Throw the birthday cake!

SEAN: And what about food fights in your mummy and daddy's home?

ALL: [Silence]

SEAN: What would you think if a friend came to your house and started throwing food all round your mummy and daddy's sitting room and the sofa got cream cake all over it?

ALL: [Silence]

GIRL (after a while): Mummy would tell us off.

LITTLE BOY (authoritatively): You just have food fights at other people's houses. Not mummy and daddy's.

SEAN (nodding): I see. So it's OK to make a mess and upset other people's houses, but not your own?
GIRL (shaking her head): That's not nice.
LITTLE BOY (pause): No … so let's have food fights at school!

Working on this book with Sean has reaffirmed my belief that manners are incredibly important. I don't know whether it's a 'living in London thing' or an 'I'm getting older and less tolerant' thing, but nowadays people don't seem to be as bothered about being polite to one another as they used to be, especially when they're dealing with strangers. And I find that rather soulless and sad. We're not blind to what goes on around us, no matter how busy we are dealing with our own lives. If someone's rude or if they ignore us when we clearly need help – and that includes something as simple as holding a door open for us if we're carrying bags or pushing a pushchair – it does affect us and put a general downer on our mood. So Sean's simple lessons on how and why we should say 'please', 'thank you', 'sorry' and 'excuse me' might seem obvious, but they seem to be necessary, as are his lessons on basic table manners when we're sharing a meal with other people. And I've found the way he teaches his classes as important as what he teaches. He's fun and easy-going, and he always gives a reason for everything. It is these elements that make his classes a success, and these elements that we have tried to focus on in the book.

I have seen Sean work his magic not only in his classes and in the research we ran for the book, but also in my own home when he helped me deal with one of my son Lucas's most annoying habits. Lucas was eighteen months old, and during every meal he had a bad habit of wiping his mouth on his sleeve. I tried to stop him doing this, but it seemed to be impossible and I was going through tubs of Vanish like there was no tomorrow. When this came up in conversation, Sean casually asked me if I gave Lucas a napkin or kitchen towel at mealtimes. A napkin? For an eighteen-month-old toddler? I wasn't convinced but I said I'd give it a go.

Well, I showed him what to do and wondered what would happen. The first piece of kitchen towel was torn up into little pieces. The second was thrown on the floor, and so was the third. I was just about to give up after a couple of days of this when, to my amazement, he finally copied me. I couldn't believe it. No more tomato stains and feeling like a washing powder commercial! And the great thing was, I didn't have to go through a cold war to get him to do it; I simply had to show him, repeatedly and without judgement, what to do.

When we started writing this book, Sean and I wanted to make sure that it covered all the topics that parents with children in the six- to twelve-year-old age bracket believed to be important. We also decided to road-test each chapter on both parents and children. We've had great fun doing this, and over twenty research groups and countless interviews later, I'd like to think we've made this book as fun and as relevant as we hoped it could be.

I hope you have as much fun reading this book together with your children as we did writing it.

Sue Carr
June 2005

Introduction

When Sue and I first talked about writing this book, I was slightly wary. I have been so careful to make sure the 'etiquette' classes I hold at the Lanesborough Hotel, London, are fun and relevant to the society we live in today that I didn't want the book to be anything less than that. A book that promoted a strict, old-fashioned concept of good manners would, in my mind, be a huge step backwards, because, while I am convinced that children need to be taught how to behave and that some of us have forgotten the basics of good manners, we also have to realise that things have moved on.

Perhaps, before we go any further, I should tell you why I started teaching children the rudiments of good manners, because it wasn't something I set out to do. In fact, when I was first asked to start the classes, I wasn't convinced there was truly a need for them.

It all began six years ago at the Lanesborough Hotel, where I am still head butler. We had some regular guests from America staying with us, who I knew quite well. On this particular occasion their children were behaving very badly in the dining room: bouncing on sofas, complaining they hadn't been bought a present, chucking cushions around the room and generally causing a bit of a stir. I felt genuinely sorry for the parents, who were obviously embarrassed and upset by their children's behaviour, so, to try to alleviate the tension, I took the children to another table and started talking them through each bit of cutlery, explaining what it was for, how to lay a table and so forth. To my relief, they not only listened, but actually seemed to enjoy themselves.

The family asked if I could give their children some more pointers about dining etiquette, and, over the ensuing weeks, other guests who'd heard about what was happening asked if their children could join in. Then London-based families who regularly dined at the hotel began to call and request tuition, and it wasn't long before I found myself putting classes into my diary as a monthly event.

I remember the first official class as if it were yesterday. I was incredibly nervous: there is no greater critic than a child. They look at you in that way that says 'perform or you're dead!', especially when they are somewhere *not* of their own volition. The first five or six classes were as much a learning curve for me as for them. To be honest, I was truly shocked by how little these children knew about good manners. I had reasoned that because most of the children came from well-off, often aristocratic, families they would know the basics, but I couldn't have been more wrong. Some ate fast food so often they didn't know how to use a knife and fork (and I'm talking about eight-year-olds). Others said they felt awkward sitting at a table because they were used to having TV dinners, and as a result they found the idea of making conversation while eating rather bizarre.

Now, I can't keep telling you how passionate I am that a family should sit down for at least one meal together every day. It doesn't matter for how long, and it doesn't matter whether it's in the kitchen or the dining room, because mealtimes aren't purely about food; they're also about conversation. They're a time for discussion – even argument – which is where my feelings about 'etiquette' veer away from the Victorian and Edwardian ideal of children sitting around the dining table looking incredibly prim and proper and only speaking when they're spoken to. To me that's a horrendous idea.

Looking back on my own childhood, I remember that my parents were incredibly strict, my father perhaps more so than my mother. He found it inexcusable not to be punctual, so if we were ever late sitting down at the table for dinner we were simply not served any food. He was a stickler for holding your knife and fork correctly, and we had to lay the table just so for every meal. If we didn't, we were sent outside and told to get on with one of the most unpopular jobs on the farm – mine was milking cows. And yet, despite all that, I have very, very fond memories of mealtimes as a child because we had great discussions, huge disagreements and lots of laughs.

My brothers and sisters and I were children who were seen and definitely heard. It was only later in life that I realised our parents had given us a great gift. Through what seemed at the time to be their constant nagging and badgering about what and how to do, say, wear, eat and so on, they gave us a confidence we took with us wherever we went. Whoever we were with, we could be confident enough never to question that our behaviour and our manners were as they should be.

Some people would like to argue that by treating us the way they did, my parents quashed our individuality, imprisoned us in an old-fashioned belief system that leaves no room for personality. Well, I couldn't disagree more. In truth they gave us freedom.

We are an image-conscious society, and we are judged by our actions in public. If you're a girl on a first date and the boy turns up wearing a smelly old sweatshirt and scruffy trainers, you wonder how much he likes you because it doesn't look like he's made an effort. If he talks with his mouth full and stuffs food into his face like he hasn't eaten for days, it doesn't exactly endear him to you. If it's your wedding and not everyone has replied, you feel embarrassed that you have to chase people up and rather hurt that they don't seem to be attaching much importance to the fact that it's your big day. And if you've hosted a party, it makes you feel good when you receive a thank-you letter from one of your guests, and when you look back and think how that person spilt red wine on your sofa, doesn't it put a soft edge around a rather horrendous memory?

In my twenty-five years in the business of butlering, I have seen people in crucially important situations – perhaps high-powered business lunches, or the first meeting with the in-laws – behave in ways that really let them down. I really felt for one incredibly well-known and successful businessman when he came for a power lunch at the hotel and proceeded to try and woo his prospective business partner with charm and wit while he drank from his finger bowl. And then there was the time when a young man was dining with his prospective in-laws and, to show his importance, grandly and loudly shouted at the waiters and clicked his fingers. His in-laws were not impressed.

But if we do not teach our children basic good manners, how can they be expected to behave properly as adults?

To know the difference between a dessert and a soup spoon, to do simple things like bother to reply to an invitation – in good time – to know that it's rude to accept an invitation and then 'bin it' in favour of a better one, to say 'thank you' to a waiter who serves you your food, or a simple 'excuse me' to someone on a train when you want to go past them – these to me are all simple acts of courtesy that should be taught to every child.

Over the last three years I have had the pleasure of listening to and teaching over three hundred or so children. As they have told me more and more about their lifestyles, I have begun to understand why they have no idea of basic good manners. Quite simply, they have never been taught them. In some instances their lives don't require them. Why learn how to set a table, for example, when you never sit at one? Why say thank you to a waiter if your parents never bother to? Why learn to eat with your mouth shut if the only thing looking at you is the TV? Why use a knife and fork when you only ever eat pizzas or hamburgers?

I have been asked in interviews recently whether some of the social 'displays' of good manners aren't old hat. My answer is that, yes, I do think some of the older 'rules' are past it and no longer relevant for our lives or society as a whole. But there are other lessons that are still very pertinent today, many of which we often don't bother with or have even forgotten. These are the lessons I cover in my classes, and that I have included in this book – the things I consider basic good manners.

In the past two years Sue and I have carried out countless research groups and interviews to try to make sure that we not only address the most popular questions and issues that affect parents with children in the six-to-twelve age bracket but also make each chapter fun as well as informative.

Since my work with these groups, I am more passionate than ever in my belief that teaching our children some sort of social code of behaviour is as imperative for their happiness in childhood as it is for their happiness in later adult life. I see children with no routine, no boundaries and no structure to their lives, and I can't help but feel that is not a good thing. Not because of an old-fashioned, fuddy-duddy idea that children need to be strictly disciplined, but because in general these children appear a little lost. In my experience, children need boundaries to know who they are and where they belong.

I firmly believe it is up to us – parents, guardians and god-parents alike – to ensure that we give our children a good start in life. And that includes giving them the confidence and self-assurance to know that wherever they go, at whatever time in their life, they don't feel uncomfortable or insecure because they're not sure how to behave.

To me, good manners give you access to all areas.

This book is not a quick fix – nor are the classes I teach. Some parents come to me expecting miracles. As they sit in the class ignoring my request to save any questions till last, talking loud-ly, smoking and generally behaving with little regard for the people around them, they expect to see their children trans-mogrify into angels. If only miracles were that easy!

I realised very early on 'Do as I say, not as I do' doesn't pull the wool over any child's eyes. I hope that you and your children have fun experimenting with and practising the points we cover, and enjoy the games and quizzes I've included from my classes.

The most important thing to remember is that this book is supposed to be fun. So please, set the right mood before you start, and sit down only when you know you've put aside enough time to enjoy the chapter together at an easy pace. Because if there is one thing *I* have learnt from teaching these classes, it is

 that to keep a child's attention, you have to give him yours.

Sean Davoren
June 2005

How to get the best out of this book

We have really tried hard to make sure that the fun, relaxed atmosphere of my classes is replicated in this book, but we need your help to get the message across. Below are some of the points that came out of the research groups we carried out. We hope you find our suggestions useful.

- When you get to the children's sections, share the reading with your child. We found older children liked to share it page by page, while younger children liked to dip in and out. Sharing the reading makes your child feel more involved – and more likely to take note.

- When you're reading the book sit side by side. Children like the closeness – and it's easier to share the book.

- Read 'A note to the grown-up' before you sit down to go through a chapter with your child. This tells you what props are needed and gives you an idea of what we're intending to achieve. Allow thirty to forty minutes for each children's section.

- Children saw these chapters as a special time they could spend with their mother or father. If you have more than one child, it's a good idea to run through the chapter with no more than two children at a time. If you can achieve it, one child at a time is ideal, especially if your children's ages are at either extreme of the age bracket (six to twelve years).

- Try to start each chapter from a position of fun. This is not an exam, and if children feel under pressure, they are less likely to listen.

Meet the Johnson family

To illustrate our story, we want to introduce you to the Johnson family who will appear throughout the book.

Robbie Johnson: Robbie is twelve years old. He loves playing rugby and only really gets grumpy when his brother and sisters borrow his things without asking.

Angelica Johnson: Angelica is eight years old. Playing tricks on Harry is one of her favourite pastimes. She loves Starbucks caramel frappuccinos and pretending to be a pop star.

Jen Johnson: Jen is ten years old. She loves celebrity gossip and is at her happiest when her mother takes her to Top Shop.

Harry Johnson: Harry is six years old. He loves dinosaurs and football and has a very bad habit of picking his nose.

Susie and Jeremy Johnson: Mum and Dad. Susie loves going to Top Shop with Jen and Angelica (except when Jen tells her she's too old to wear some of the stuff). Jeremy is at his happiest when he's at a rugby match with Harry and Robbie, or reading his paper. He has a bad habit of picking chips from other people's plates.

You will also meet these other members of the family: Auntie Sarah, who is Susie's sister. Auntie Sarah has no children but believes all children should be respected and treated like adults and keeps on asking her nephews and nieces: 'How are you? How do you *feel*? No, but how are you – *really*?'

Grandma Johnson: Jeremy's mother. She loves having the family for Sunday lunch but has a bad habit of overcooking cabbage.

Mutt the dog: Mutt is worried that if the children learn about good manners they'll stop feeding him under the table at mealtimes.

Chapter 1

As easy as one, two, three

A note to the grown-ups

This chapter is all about showing children the importance of basic courtesy and how they can make a positive difference to someone else's day – as well as their own. Children, especially younger ones, are egocentric. We all are, really, but as we get older we (hopefully) realise that it's not one of the more socially acceptable attributes we were born with and we learn to think about how we are making the people around us feel. Part of a parent's job is to take the time to teach their children the importance of looking outside themselves, and show them how they have the power to affect other people's lives for better or worse. You can bet your bottom dollar that if a child is rude and disrespectful, they've learnt it from ... *their parents*.

Let me give you a couple of examples.

One young man, aged about ten, was staying at the hotel with his parents. 'Get me an orange juice!' he shouted at a member of my staff. His mother looked on fondly, pleased, I think, that her child was 'asserting himself'. When the boy tasted his orange juice, he looked at me, shouted, 'I don't like this,' and threw the glass of orange juice in my face. His parents ignored what had happened. It turned out that the boy didn't like fresh orange juice with the 'bits' in it.

On another occasion, a young girl aged about seven was staying in the hotel with her parents. The young girl decided that she wanted to have the furniture in her room moved around. Now, I always want a guest to be comfortable – my maxim is, just as long as it's legal, I'll do it – so we started moving the furniture around for her. Her parents looked on as she pointed and shouted, 'Move my bed! Get me a DVD and a different TV! Put that table there! No not there, *there*.' This went on for a good three-quarters of an hour without a please or a thank you in sight. The young girl screamed when she felt my assistant hadn't listened to her: 'I said, stupid, I want my bed moved *there*!'

What amazed me was that her parents didn't say a word. They actually looked proud of their daughter. They *were* proud, because they felt they had taught her a valuable lesson – how to take control of a situation and get things done. They didn't care that she had shown no respect for the other people in the room. They didn't care that her behaviour was inconsiderate. And how could I, or any of the staff, take a dislike to the girl for behaving the way she did? As far as she was concerned she was simply doing what her parents had told her to do. The most frightening aspect of this story is that, because of her parents' reaction, *the young girl honestly believed she was doing the right thing*.

These may seem extreme examples, but they illustrate the importance of a few basic words that I believe our modern society cannot function happily without: please, thank you, sorry, excuse me, hello and goodbye.

So in this chapter I take you and your child through…

• My list of 'Important Words'.

• Why and when these words should be used.

Our main aim in this chapter is to try to show your child how, by simply remembering to use these small but important words – like saying thank you to a waiter, or please to a cashier at the supermarket – they can make a big, positive difference to how people feel, and to how people feel *about them*.

The best way to help your child remember these lessons is to show them how *you* use the 'Important Words' in your normal, daily life. I'd pick one word every day, and while you're out with the children, really focus on using it when it's appropriate, and praise your children when you hear them use it.

As you go through the children's section that follows, please remember there's no rush. In our experience, it's better to let the conversation flow, occasionally wandering off at a tangent, than

to plough through the section stoically word by word as if it's a chore that needs to be done.

As easy as one, two, three

It's amazing how one person – you – can make such a difference to people's lives. You've got a choice. You can behave in a nice way, speak politely, be helpful and kind and make people smile. Or you can shout and stamp to make sure you get what you want.

The first choice means people like to be with you, invite you to their houses, help you when you're stuck and, because you make them feel nice, they make *you* feel nice. The second choice means … well, would you like to be around someone like that?

Behaving like the first sort of person is not that hard. It doesn't take much. It all comes down to 'manners', a few simple dos and don'ts that mean your behaviour doesn't offend people and make them feel fed up with you. Now, you might think 'manners' is a boring word that spoils your fun. Actually, having good manners is like having a key to a door that makes the world a nicer place to live in, not just for the people around you, but for *you*.

In this book, I'm going to show you a few simple things that give you that key. I'm also going to show you that it's not boring or hard work or like being in trouble at school to learn about good manners. It's actually quite fun.

Let's think of some examples that show how bad manners can upset people. For example, let's say your parents have just said 'no' to you about something. Maybe you wanted to go out with friends, or you wanted a new toy, and the answer's just come back – a definite and absolute 'no'.

What do you do?

Well, a lot of children I know get grumpy and sulk, and they make sure that everyone knows they're fed up. They refuse to smile at people, even if those people are trying to help them. They don't say please. They don't say thank you. In fact, they're so into thinking about what *they* want and how *they* feel, that they don't even realise that they are not acting in a nice way to the people around them and they could be hurting other people's feelings.

I know other children – like Harry and Angelica – who get so excited when they visit the cinema or an amusement park that they run ahead at breakneck speed, crashing into people, pushing to the head of the queue and bashing smaller children out of the way, because all they're thinking is, 'I want to be first on the Raging River!' or 'I want to sit at the front!' They never once think that if they said, 'Excuse me', people would let them go past happily, without feeling hurt or ignored.

A few small words

Good manners start with a few very important words. They are so simple that you probably know them already, but you probably haven't ever thought about them much, or how important they really are. They're almost magical, because the difference they make to yours and other people's day-to-day life is quite incredible. They make people smile, they get you invited to parties and people's homes, people like you for using them, and whenever you do use them people always go out of their way to help you.

Now, that doesn't sound too bad, does it?

I bet you can guess which words are on my list, but the question to ask yourself is: *Do you actually use them?*

Why should I use them?

Please

If you want something, or if you want someone to help you with something, adding a 'please' to the beginning or end of your sentence makes your request *sound* like a request, not a demand.

Look at the example on the next page. Which sounds better to you?

You see how childish Harry sounds in the first version and how grown-up and in control he sounds in the second?

Top tip!

Shouting isn't the best way to ask for something. It just makes people cross. How do you feel when people shout at you? Talking in your normal voice, not screeching and whining, is the best way to get people to listen to you.

By the way, I'm not promising that just because you say 'please' you'll automatically get what you want! But what I can promise you is that if you say please, people will act warmly towards you and will be more likely to hear you out.

Thank You

If you gave a friend a present, and they took it from you and didn't bother to say thank you, how would you feel?

If you held a door open for someone and they walked straight through and ignored you, how would you feel?

If an old lady dropped her shopping and you helped her pick her things up, and she didn't say thank you, what would you think? I'd think 'What a rude lady! Someone should teach her a few manners!'

Whenever someone does something to you that is kind or thoughtful, make the effort to say 'thank you' to them. They'll feel appreciated, and, you never know, they might want to do nice things for you in the future.

Top tip!

Grown-ups can be rude and bad-mannered too. If a grown-up is rude to you, remind them – politely – that words like 'please' and 'thank you' are there for grown-ups to use as much as children.

Sorry

This is one of the most difficult words for grown-ups and children to say. Nobody likes to admit that they've done something naughty or wrong, or that they didn't behave in a very nice way. But if you have, or you've hurt someone's feelings, the best thing to do is take a deep breath and say *sorry*. It goes quite a long way towards making things all right again.

Sorry is also a good word to use when you bump into people accidentally, or tread on people's toes. Bothering to say 'sorry' shows that you actually *care*. The person whose toe is

throbbing will appreciate the fact that you made the effort and not feel so bad about it.

None of us likes to fall out with our friends. It's horrible when you've had cross words with someone and you ignore each other, both of you sure that it was the other person's fault. The fact is that when two people argue, they have normally *both* said something that wasn't very nice. So have a think about what you said, be big and be the first to say sorry. You'll probably find that the other person is relieved and says sorry too. But even if they don't, at least you can sleep well that night, knowing you did the right thing.

Top tip!

If you say 'sorry', make sure you mean it. People can tell if you're saying 'sorry' without actually feeling sorry!

Top tip!

If you say sorry to a friend and they'd don't say sorry back (but they said some things to you that weren't very nice), remember that you can't get anyone to say sorry if they don't want to. The one thing to remember is that you've been the cool one and behaved in a very grown-up way.

Excuse Me

Look at the illustration on the next page. Angelica and Harry haven't quite got the point, have they? Yes, they're saying 'excuse me', but look at the trouble they're causing! Whether you say 'Excuse me', or not, pushing in is a definite no-no.

But let's say you're shopping with your parents, and the store you're in is really busy. One minute you're all walking together, the next you've become separated. Of course you want to find your parents, and maybe you feel a bit worried

and want to push people out of the way, but now is the time to say 'Excuse me'. Say it firmly and loudly to make sure they hear you, especially if it's noisy in the store. If they don't hear you, quickly touch their elbow to get their attention and push gently forward, explaining you need to get to your parents.

Top tip!

People are far happier to move out of your way if they know why you want them to move out of your way. As well as saying 'Excuse me', let them know what you're trying to do.

Sometimes people are not aware that they're standing in your way. If they're lost or looking at a map, they're probably not concentrating on what's going on around them. Again, a simple 'Excuse me' should be enough for them to realise they are getting in your way and they'll move.

'Excuse me' is also a great way to interrupt people *nicely*. Have you noticed that if you just start talking at someone when they're talking with someone else, it simply *doesn't work*. Have you ever thought why? Well, first of all they don't hear the first bit of what you're saying because they're busy concentrating on the other person. Secondly, you've annoyed them so much they don't want to listen. How can anyone listen to two people talking at the same time? So before you say *anything*, say, 'Excuse me, Grandma,' or whoever you want to talk to. This lets them know that you want to interrupt them, and gives them time to finish what they're saying or doing before they switch their focus to you. Then you can say the rest.

Top tip!

If there is a queue, don't push through to the front – no matter how small you are!

Hello and Goodbye

These two are maybe the most obvious words on the list, but guess what – even these get forgotten. (I have to be honest and tell you it drives me bananas when people don't use them. It sounds so rude!)

Look at all the different ways in which Robbie and the gang pick up the phone:

There are two simple reasons why you should say hello when you pick up the phone. It lets people know you're there, and it sounds friendly.

The two reasons for saying goodbye at the end are just the same.

The other day, I was on the phone to a mother in Los Angeles who was calling me to make sure there was room in one of my classes for her daughter. We must have chatted for a

good fifteen minutes, and then she said, 'Great, we'll see you there.' Then the receiver was slammed down and the line went dead.

Had she dropped the phone? Had we been cut off? No, she just didn't say 'Goodbye'.

It felt so odd not having the comfort of hearing a polite 'Goodbye' to know that we had finished our conversation. And it felt incredibly rude. How much time does it take to say 'Goodbye'? Think what it means; 'good'-bye. It's a well-wish, and it makes us feel good when we hear it. And from a practical point of view it tells both of us we've reached the end of our conversation.

Top tip!

If you ever think you can't be bothered to say 'thank you' or wonder if it's worth saying 'sorry', think how you'd feel in the same situation – say you're the person who has given a present and not been thanked, or the person with the drink spilt over them. You wouldn't be feeling too happy about it, would you?

29

Game

Which Word Goes Where?

Robbie and Angelica are arguing. Robbie's going to the cinema with Jennifer and her friend Mai (who Robbie thinks is rather nice). Because Mai is going, Robbie wants to wear his favourite jumper, so he looks good. Angelica wants to go to the cinema but she's not old enough, so she's hidden Robbie's jumper. If she can't go, then she doesn't want Robbie to – she wants him to stay and watch the DVD about a haunted house. Which words can be used to fill the blanks?

Please   Sorry   Thank you   Hi   'Bye   Excuse me

ROBBIE: Angelica, ... give me my jumper!

ANGELICA: Only if I can come to the cinema with you.

ROBBIE: You're not old enough.

ANGELICA: I *am*!

ROBBIE: No you're not! What's that under your duvet?

ANGELICA (leaning back, stopping him getting to her bed):
  Nothing!

ROBBIE (kneeling down): Angelica, ... listen to me.
  You're not allowed to go to the cinema, but I will watch the
  DVD with you when I get back – if you give me my jumper
  back.

ANGELICA: You promise?

ROBBIE: Promise.

(Angelica sighs. Goes
to her doll's pram,
picks out his jumper
and gives it to him.)

ROBBIE: .... So
  what's under your duvet?

ANGELICA: That's Jen's...

JENNIFER: .... everyone! We've
  got to get going, we're going to be
  late. Has anyone seen my handbag?

ANGELICA (to Robbie): .... I hid
  your jumper.

ROBBIE: That's OK. ....
  See you later.

ANGELICA: Have a good time! Now (turning to Jen), what's that about your handbag?

JENNIFER (looking suspicious): You've hidden it, haven't you!

ANGELICA: You can have it back if I can come to the cinema with you.

JENNIFER: ANGELICA!!! (Jennifer races after her).

ANGELICA: ....!!!! (as she barges past Harry in the hallway).

Before you go...

Pick one of my important words to practise using for the rest of the day, ideally the one you most often forget to use.

Chapter 2

So what's wrong with fingers?

A note to the grown-ups

It was only when Elizabeth I came to the throne that cutlery*
became chic at the royal court. Up until then a large carving knife

*The word cutlery is derived from the old French word *coutel* = knife. *Coutel* is
itself derived from the Latin *culter* = knife or ploughshare. *Concise Oxford English
Dictionary*

and a dirty hand were de rigueur. So if Henry VIII pooh-poohed using a knife and fork, why do we expect a child to act any differently?

The fact is that children see knives, forks and spoons as cumbersome. Rather than seeing them as useful implements, they see them as a bother, as a pain in the proverbial. They get nagged to use them, but are given no particular reason *why* they should use them. It might seem obvious to you that a fork is very useful for holding a piece of food in place as you cut it, or that because a bread knife is flat and doesn't have a serrated edge it's ideally designed to spread butter on to a bread roll, or that eating food with cutlery instead of fingers is more hygienic and less messy, but this rationale is not obvious to children. It needs to be explained to them.

It also needs to be demonstrated.

One delightful little girl, aged eight, came to one of my classes. Her parents were regular guests at the hotel and they were genuinely concerned that their child did not know how to hold a knife and fork. *Aged eight, and she didn't know how to use a knife and fork?* I couldn't quite believe it. I thought it was probably more a case of the little girl not *wanting* to use a knife and fork, but after spending a morning with her, I realised I was wrong.

Now, I have no doubt that this child was loved by her parents, but the problem was, both parents were incredibly busy and spent a good portion of the year travelling, which meant that the young girl and her sibling often ate in the kitchen with the staff, sitting at the worktop, watching television. And to make sure the children ate their food and didn't whine, the cook would give them any food they fancied, namely, by the sounds of it, pizza, pizza with fries, pizza with sausages and the odd smattering of a cheese sandwich or two. Why did this little girl *need* to know how to hold a knife and fork? They weren't required in her normal, day-to-day life. It was only when her parents occasionally took her out for lunch that she was expected to use cutlery. Sadly, these outings, from what I could gather, seldom had a happy ending as the parents simply became increasingly irritated as the lunch progressed and the young girl studiously ignored her cutlery and tried to use her fingers. They would nag at her all through the meal, which would give her another reason to think 'Why bother?'

I have found that once children *hear* or *are shown* a reason for doing something, they're normally more amenable to *listening*, and to trying it out.

In this chapter we're going to be looking at the basics of table etiquette – and even if you and your children think you know what the basics are, it's worth going through them again. I will talk you and your child through:

- Recognising the different pieces of cutlery you'll find on a dining table.

- What each particular piece of cutlery is used for.

- How to lay a table.

In the next chapter we deal with the easy way to hold different pieces of cutlery, so try to keep this chapter to *recognising* which bit of cutlery does what and where it 'lives' on the table. As always, don't expect your children to remember exactly what's what straight away. The information is always here for them to refer back to, but the best way forward is to reinforce the information and keep showing them by example on a day-to-day basis. That's the only way information will eventually stick.

Props

Before you invite your child to begin reading this chapter with you, lay two places at the table, side by side.

A full table setting is shown below. It's up to you to decide whether your child is at an age to learn a basic setting (for a three-course meal) or a full setting (for a four-course meal). For a basic setting, simply remove the fish fork and knife.

For a basic setting, you will need:

2 large knives, 2 bread knives (or 2 small knives), 2 large forks, 2 side plates, 2 dinner plates, 2 soup bowls, 2 soup spoons, 2 dessert spoons, 2 dessert forks (small forks), 2 napkins (or paper serviettes or kitchen towel, it really doesn't matter), 2 water glasses (and, if you wish, a white wine glass and red wine glass), a jug of water.

If you use the same-sized spoons for dessert and soup, the same-sized forks for your main meal and pudding, and the same glasses for white and red wine, do as you would at home and place them in both settings.

Both settings shown are correct, so use the one that you prefer. In Victorian days, the dessert fork and knife were always placed at the head of the setting and it was left to the butler to 'draw' the dessert cutlery down to the side after the dishes and cutlery from the main dish had been cleared away. Nowadays, butlers and housekeepers are an endangered species, so unfortunately we are not always there to help you.

Top tip!

We found in our research groups that sometimes the conversation would go off on all sorts of tangents, and I would suggest, within reason, that you let it. A lot of the time we found that both adult and child learnt something from it.

Top tip!

When you're laying a setting for a child, give them a glass that is light enough for them to lift. If I have very young children staying at the Lanesborough, I always put a straw in a small glass to help them.

Top tip!

Why not give your child the responsibility of laying the table for Sunday lunch, or breakfast? They'll love the sense of being trusted and having an important job to do.

And please remember, after reading this chapter, that if you immediately revert to TV dinners, forget about napkins, don't bother laying the table, use only a fork for eating in front of your children and end up making your life easier by giving your child only food that doesn't require cutlery, everything they have learnt will quickly be forgotten.

So what's wrong with fingers?

Side plate: it's smaller than a dinner plate, and you'll find it to the left.
Red wine glass: it's larger than the white wine glass.
White wine glass: smaller than the red wine glass and furthest away
from you.
Water glass: this is the glass closest to you.
Napkin: you'll find your napkin either on your side plate, or in a glass, or
on your dinner plate.
Dessert spoon and fork: sometimes you'll just be given a spoon.

I'm sure you know what a knife and fork are for. They're certainly not for picking your nose! And I think any manicurist worth
her salt would have a fit if she saw you poking your dainty nails
with a fork!

Knives and forks have one use only, and that is to help us
eat our food. And, despite what you may think, they do make
eating easier. The fork holds the food in position while the
knife cuts it. And why do we need to cut our food? Well, have
you ever tried putting a whole sirloin steak in your mouth? In

this country, unlike others such as China and Japan, our meat and fish dishes are generally served whole, and this is why our cutlery is geared towards cutting and holding our food in place.

But these aren't the only pieces of cutlery you'll find on a dining table. Have a look at the table setting that has been beautifully laid out for you. Do you know which is the soup spoon? The dessert spoon? Do you know why they have different shaped heads? It's the usual reason – to help make eating easier.

Let's go through things one by one.

What's what on the table

The **soup spoon** is deliberately designed to hold liquid. It's deeper and wider than a dessert spoon, and it's not meant to be put in your mouth. If you've got one in front of you, try and put it in your mouth. It's not easy, is it? That's because a soup spoon is designed for you to *pour* the soup into your mouth, using the *side*, not the tip, of the spoon (the side of the spoon touches your lips, and you gently pour the soup into your mouth). Pouring the soup means you don't end up burning your mouth with a whole spoonful of soup. And as an added benefit, it's a little more difficult to slurp with a soup spoon.

Slurping is what happens when you use a dessert spoon for soup.

The **dessert spoon** is not meant to be used for soup – it's meant to be used for more substantial food such as puddings, ice cream or cake, food that you can't pour into your mouth.

The dessert spoon *is* meant to be put in your mouth, which is why it's longer and thinner than the soup spoon. Unlike the soup spoon, you put the dessert spoon in your mouth *tip first*. Sometimes there will be a dessert fork laid opposite the dessert spoon. Dessert forks look exactly like normal dinner forks, they're just smaller.

Slurping competition

Pick up the water jug and pour some water into your soup bowls. Pretend the water is soup. Try eating it, first with a dessert spoon, then with a soup spoon.

Try slurping! Which spoon makes it easier to pour water into your mouth? And which one is easier to slurp with? Who between you can make the largest and longest slurp?

There is one other knife that has been laid out in front of you that we haven't yet talked about.

The knife on the side plate is called a **bread knife**. If you've got one in front of you, pick it up and have a look at it. How is a bread knife different from a normal dinner knife?

The bread knife is always placed on your side plate. It's wide and flat to help you spread butter, and it doesn't have a serrated edge because it doesn't need one. The only thing a bread knife needs to do is spread the butter over your bread roll. In the olden days you had to cut your bread roll with a knife, but nowadays, we're much more European in the way we eat food, so it's absolutely fine to tear it with your fingers.

Other knives you might see on a table

A fish knife. If you order fish, you might be given a fish knife.

The fish knife is used for all fish dishes and is especially useful for eating boned fish. The pointy tip of the knife helps you lift the skin off the fish, and the flatness of the knife is great for skimming the flesh of the fish off the bone.

Top tip!

There is nothing more annoying than getting a mouth full of fish bones when you're eating fish. If you don't feel confident about eating a boned fish, it is perfectly polite to ask the waiter in the restaurant, or a grown-up, to prepare your fish 'off the bone', which basically means you get all the nice bits without the hassle.

The butter knife. Well, three guesses what this knife is used for!

Its pointy tip is perfect for cutting off a piece of butter and then placing it on your plate. Why have a butter knife? Well, imagine you're eating your Sunday lunch and there's gravy on your knife and you stick your knife in the butter dish to pick up some butter, and the gravy goes on the butter. The next morning you fancy some butter and jam, so you pick up some butter from the butter dish, spread it all over your toast and then bite into ... yesterday's gravy! A butter knife means the butter stays clean and doesn't taste of anything but butter.

The **cheese knife** has a dual purpose. First, the sharp or serrated edge helps you cut through the slice of cheese that you are helping yourself to. Second, the pointy bit at the end enables you to pick the cheese up and carry it on to your plate. Cutting cheese can be quite hard, so ask a grown-up for help. And if you don't know what sort of cheese you are being offered, *ask*. Some cheeses look innocent, but in fact they're not only smelly, but they taste of old socks!

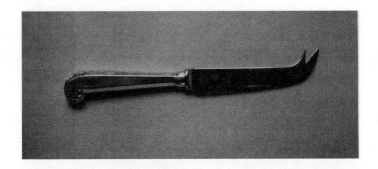

The **steak knife** is pointed and specifically designed for cutting all different types of steak. It has an obvious serrated edge and is incredibly sharp.

Napkins

Napkins make sure that you don't go to school with the left-overs of your breakfast on your face or your clothes. I don't think it matters if your napkin is made out of cotton or kitchen towel. The most important thing is that you use one.

If you look back at the illustration, you'll see that there's no one place on the table where the napkin is placed. When you sit down at your family dining table, you should pick up your napkin before you start eating. If you're under eight, you can tuck your napkin into your shirt or the neck of your dress if you like. If you're over eight, unfold your napkin and place it over your lap.

If you need to excuse yourself from the table, simply pick up your napkin and either leave it on your chair or place it on your side plate.

Just so you know, 'napkin' is usually the word used to describe napkins made out of linen or cotton. 'Serviette' is the word used to describe a napkin made out of paper.

The mixed-up memory game

Now that we've been through each piece of cutlery, why don't you have a go at laying the table yourself?

Put the dinner plates, glasses, soup bowls and napkins to one side. Now, put your hands on the table, and *mix up all the cutlery*. Make it a total mess. Push all the pieces of cutlery together into one confused pile. Perfect!

Now, taking your time, lay your own table setting. If you get stuck, just look at the illustration on page 39.

As you become more used to where all the pieces of cutlery, glasses and crockery go, you can race each other to see who can lay a table setting in the quickest amount of time. Waiters I work with can lay a table for twelve people in a record four minutes (that's with the tablecloth down and all the cutlery already polished). That's 30 seconds per setting. When you become expert at it, see if you can match their record.

Hint: I'd start by placing the dinner plate in the centre, so you have the plate to work around.

Dinner plates and cutlery are placed about a thumb's length in from the edge of the table (so you don't knock any of it off the table when you sit up or get down), and all cutlery, apart from the dessert spoon and dessert fork, should be pointing to six o'clock. (Go back to the illustration if you want to check.)

Escape routes from tricky situations:

Below are the top three tricky situations concerning cutlery that children have told me about. I hope you find my answers useful.

- *If you're faced with lots of different pieces of cutlery* and you don't know which piece to pick up first, this rhyme will help you:
  Forks and spoons and knives a spin,
  Always work from outside in!
  If you always start with the cutlery that has been placed furthest away from the dinner plate, and move inwards for each course, you can't go wrong. If there's any cutlery above the dinner plate, this is always used last.

- *If you drop a piece of cutlery on the floor* – when you're out at a restaurant, draw the waiter's attention to the piece of cutlery that has fallen. As he's the one who has to kneel down and pick it up, a little smile or a quick apology would be nice. If you're at a friend's house, pick up the fallen piece of cutlery, tell a grown-up what's happened (again with a quick apology), and they'll happily replace it with a clean piece.

- *If you're unsure what a piece of cutlery is for – ask!* There's nothing wrong in asking, and no one will mind.

Before you go...

Tell each other three new things that you have learnt from reading this chapter.

Chapter 3

Hold on! The easy way to use knives, forks and spoons

A note to the grown-ups

I'm probably stating the obvious, but as well as the easy way to use cutlery there are lots of difficult ways, and you can bet your bottom dollar that your child will take great delight in finding one of the latter. They will hold their fork too close to the bottom, try to cut their food with their knife turned the wrong way round, tear their food with a fork instead of cutting it with a knife and wield a spoon in a fist-like grip so their yoghurt goes flying in every direction apart from into their mouth. And then when they get frustrated that they can't eat with their cutlery, they'll dump the knife, dump the fork if they get really fed up, and finally resort to their firm favourites: their fingers.

And what about the times when children *aren't* using their knives and forks? When they're sitting at the table, waiting for their food to be served, wriggling in their seats and wondering what mischief will keep them entertained. In my classes, children have found the most weird and wonderful things to do with cutlery. They stab the backs of their hands to see if it hurts, take great delight in creating fork imprints on the surface of the table, decide that knives are wonderful daggers for killing dragons and attacking other 'knights' (normally their siblings), and act as if they'd never heard a musical note in their life as they drop their cutlery on to the floor with an ear-splitting clatter and a look of sheer delight on their faces.

Our job in this chapter is to help them see cutlery as a good thing, not some Herculean feat they have to overcome or walk away from deflated and defeated, and definitely not something to 'stab' their friends or engrave the table with.

In this chapter we will talk through some of the most basic yet crucial lessons a child can learn about how to eat and how to use their cutlery. We will discuss:

- The easy way to pick up, hold and use knives, forks and spoons.

- What *not* to do with cutlery.

- How to sit at a table.

- How to hold chopsticks.

> **Top Tip!**
>
> And remember, no one is perfect – it takes time and practice to perfect using a knife and fork, so the more practice your children get, and the more time you spend sharing meals with them so they can see how you use a knife and fork, the easier and quicker it will be for them to learn.

Props

You will need:
2 large knives, 2 large forks and 2 soup spoons, a jug of water, 2 plates, 2 soup bowls, 2 napkins, 2 bananas (or something soft you can practise cutting up on). You'll also need to be sitting at the table where you eat at home.

For the section on chopsticks (page 62) you'll need a pair of chopsticks each (you're going to be doing this together), 4 bowls and a mixture of food to practise on.

For beginners: you could use pieces of torn bread, chocolate squares and some pieces of apple. If your child is used to using chopsticks, try crackers, grapes and some chocolate or chewy sweets. If you decide to race each other, you could add some more tricky things to your bowl like grains of cooked rice or some raisins. (I'd suggest you put *at least* one thing in your child's bowl that is a favourite food of theirs. It really helps them focus on having a go.)

As with all the games in this book, the most important thing is to nurture your child's confidence and help them feel that they're doing a pretty good job.

You can help younger children get used to chopsticks by preparing their own pair of 'ready-to-use' chopsticks especially for them:

1. Wind a rubber band tightly around the top of both chopsticks.

2. Open them to about 45 degrees and place a thick, folded tissue snugly in between the chopsticks, fixing it in position with the band.

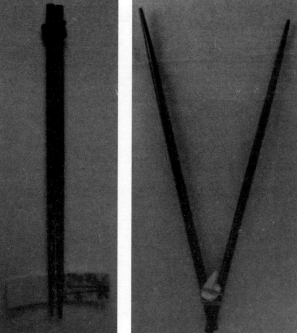

The chopsticks are now ready to use. The band holds the chopsticks in position and helps the child control their position between their fingers. You might say, why bother learning about other cutlery from around the world? Well, by teaching children about diversity, we can give them a head start in life as well as greater confidence and knowledge.

Top tip!

Make the effort to start each chapter from a position of fun. This is not a school exam – it's special time for you and your child to enjoy together. If, for some reason, your child doesn't want to try to hold their cutlery properly or to try using chopsticks, don't force them or lose your temper. Instead, carry out the examples yourself and let them watch you. The worst thing your child can feel is pressure to perform. Be patient and try again another time.

Hold on! The easy way to use knives, forks and spoons

OK, you now know all about the different types of cutlery you can find on a table. Now the question is what do you do with them? Do you stick them up your brother's or sister's nose? Do you use the back of your spoon as a mirror to check you don't have spinach between your teeth? Do you start playing pirates and pretend your knives are swords? Absolutely, completely and 100 per cent not!

And the reason why? Because knives and forks are not *toys*! They are sharp, they can be dangerous, and they were invented to be used for one thing only, and that is *eating*.

You most certainly **don't** dig the prongs of your fork into the table. You **don't** rub your fingers up and down the edge of the knife. And you **don't** fool around, pointing your cutlery at other people. Knives or forks might look harmless, but used in the wrong way they can cause accidents. How would you like it if someone started waving a fork in front of your eyes, or a friend hit you on the head with the back of their spoon? Would you laugh? If it was me, I'd get cross, because they could have hurt me. I wouldn't be happy if someone poked my eye out – and nor would you!

Top tip!

If someone is acting in a thoughtless way towards you with their cutlery and could hurt you, no matter how funny they think they're being, tell them to stop. And if they don't, go and ask a grown-up to help you. That's what grown-ups are there for.

Another thing to remember when you sit down at a table and the cutlery has already been laid out for you is that it has been washed for you. It has been cleaned and polished so that there are no bits of old, smelly food sticking to the knife, fork or spoon. And if your cutlery is clean it means there are no bad bacteria waiting to tunnel down into your stomach and give you food poisoning. So next time you sit down for a meal, only touch your cutlery when it's time to start eating, and then only touch the handles, *never* the part that touches your food.

Knives and Forks

Have a look at the picture at the beginning of this chapter, on page 48. What are Harry, Robbie, Jennifer and Angelica doing with their knives and forks? Does it look right to you?

Well, come on, Angelica! What are you going to eat up there? And Harry, it might *feel* easier to hold just a fork, but trying to cut your food with the side of a dinner fork is much more difficult and much messier than using a knife as well. And holding your fork so near the prongs doesn't really help you pick up food, it just means your fingers will get covered in food and goo. As for Jennifer, you might think you look quite cool holding your knife and fork like pens, but how are you going to cut your food or hold it in position when you can't even control your knife or fork properly? You're just making life difficult for yourself. And Robbie, you've been given a knife and fork to use, so why don't you use them?

Top tip!

Wrapping your fingers around the handles of your knife and fork make them much easier to control.

Let's see if we can use the cutlery properly.

Peel the bananas and place them (or whatever food you're practising with) on the plates in front of you, ready to practise cutting.

Before you start, just check – are you sitting properly in your chairs?

Is your cutlery laid out correctly? Check back to the illustration on page 39 if you need to.

Now:

Pick up your knife and fork from the table, using your thumb, index and middle finger.

Keep your elbows in. You're not weightlifting, and it's not great to stick your elbow in your dinner companion's face.

Hold your knife and fork slightly in front of you, with your forearms at right angles to your body.

Ease your knife into the cutting position between your thumb, index and middle finger so that the ball of the knife (the end) sits easily in the middle of the palm of your hand.

Do the same with the fork. The flat end of the fork should fit into the middle of the palm of your hand as well.

The most important question to ask yourself now is: Do I feel comfortable?

If you find that your elbows are lower than the table top, and as a result you're having to tilt your wrists up to get your cutlery in position, then your seat is too low. If you're at a friend's house or out at a restaurant when this happens, it would be good to ask an adult if they have a cushion for you to sit on. After all, eating should be a pleasure, not a circus act.

Now, decide where you're going to cut the banana. Remember you want to cut off a *bite-size* piece so it goes easily into your mouth. Big mouthfuls of food don't do you any favours. They are difficult to chew, they can make you choke, and if you swallow big, slightly chewed pieces of food, they can lie in your stomach and give you indigestion. Not to mention that a mouth filled and overflowing with food isn't exactly a pretty sight.

Top tip!

Some children and grown-ups think it's easier to eat their food just using a fork, and they don't use their knife. In my experience that's quite bananas! Because not using a knife makes the whole job of eating more difficult. And wastes time. And makes a mess of your food.

Forks need knives and knives need forks. You can't expect a fork to do the job of a knife – they're not designed to cut. You end up tearing your food and you can't control the size of the mouthful of food you want to cut off as easily. And you spend so much time chasing your food around your plate that by the time you manage to tear a chunk off, it's normally cold. So it really doesn't make sense. Use your knife too.

Stick your fork into the banana right next to where you've decided you want to make your cut. The fork will hold the banana in position and stop it skidding off the side of your plate as you cut. Hold the fork still, and firmly cut through the banana with your knife.

If you are cutting through meat, you might need to cut through it with your knife more than once. This is perfectly acceptable, and you shouldn't feel silly if you can't cut through food on your first try. Grown-ups often have to cut through food more than once to cut all the way through. Just as long as you hold the food in position with your fork so it doesn't fly off anywhere, you can have as many goes as you wish. And if you decide you've had enough and want some help, ask. There's nothing wrong in asking for help.

Spoons

Put the soup bowls in front of you and fill them with water. As you know, there are different shapes of spoon – round for soup and oval for dessert.

Hold soup and dessert spoons flat, in the crook between your thumb and fingers, at right angles to your hand.

Now, pick up your soup spoon; check you're holding it correctly (see previous page) and start to scoop the soup up, by pushing the spoon away from you (see below). If you submerge your whole spoon in your soup, the spoon gets hot – very hot – and the side of the spoon that you place next to your mouth burns your lips, whereas if you scoop the spoon away from you, only the far side of the spoon gets hot – not the side that you're going to put next to your lips.

When you've scooped, put the near side of the spoon to your lips and gently pour the soup into your mouth.

As we said in chapter 2, the dessert spoon is designed to go into your mouth, tip first. Sometimes if the dessert you're going to be given is thick and gooey, you'll be given a dessert fork and a dessert spoon. You pick up the spoon and the fork at the same time (as with the knife and fork, they work well together). Use the fork to cut your dessert into bite-size pieces and then to guide the pieces on to your spoon.

As the fork is going to be doing the cutting, I'd say put your fork in your strongest hand.

Some general rules to help you:

- When it comes to all cutlery, there's one important – and useful – thing to remember: *if you're not using it, put it down!* That way, you won't get tired of holding your cutlery, and you won't need to prop your wrists up against the table. So when you're chewing, or having a rest from eating (eating isn't a race – you don't have to gobble it all up in one go) rest your cutlery on the side of your plate, as shown below.

- If you're right handed you can rest the spoon on the right hand side of the plate, and if you're left handed, rest the spoon on the left hand side of the plate.

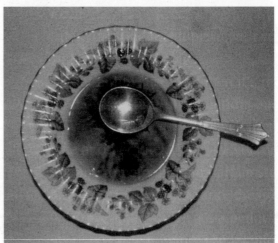

- Never bend down to the food on your plate, always keep your back straight and *use your knife and fork to bring the food to your mouth*. That way it will be easier to swallow your food, and other people won't have to spend the whole dinner looking at the top of your head.

- When you've decided you've had enough of whatever you're eating, do you know what to do with your knife and fork? And your spoon? Simply bring your knife and fork – or your spoon, or your spoon and fork – together in the half-past six position (see right). The reason for doing this is to show people that you've finished.

- By the way, if you're left handed, never feel that you have to hold your cutlery as a right handed person would. The most important thing about eating is that it feels comfortable and natural to you.

61

> ### Top tip!
>
> If the cutlery you have been given feels too heavy, ask the grown-up you're with if they have a smaller dessert fork, knife or more casual cutlery that you could use.
>
> Ask for a cushion if your elbows are lower than the table and you're not at a comfortable height to use your cutlery.

Chopsticks

Chopsticks have been around longer than we have had knives and forks. In fact they go back 5,000 years!

Have you ever tried using them?

How to become a chopstick pro

Now, one thing I'm a great believer in is that it's polite if you're trying another culture's food to at least have a go at using their cutlery. I'll let you into a secret: chopsticks are not as tricky as they look. In fact you use the same fingers you use to control your knife and fork – the forefinger, thumb and middle finger.

Have a look at the picture on the next page, but *before* you pick your chopsticks up, remember:

- Only the top chopstick ever moves

- Keep the lower chopstick fixed in position using the thumb and the forefinger

The lower down the chopstick is held, the easier it is to control (which is why Japanese chopsticks, which are shorter than Chinese chopsticks, are easier to practise with). The most difficult, but supposedly the most professional, way to hold chopsticks is to hold them near their top, so that's what you can aim for once you start feeling more confident.

Top tip!

A lady from Shanghai told me the best way to use chopsticks correctly is to pretend they are brushes painting a picture. So, rather than stabbing at your food, your hand movements should be smooth and flowing...

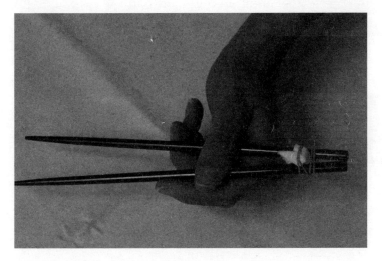

Chopstick Practice (and a good excuse to eat some sweets)
To practise using your chopsticks, set two bowls in front of you – one with food in and one empty. Try picking up each piece of food and, like a crane, lifting it up and putting it down in the other bowl. As the grown-up has probably had more experience, they can choose some slightly more tricky bits of food. As

you get more proficient, you can start racing each other – try picking up small grains of cooked rice.

Why not have a go now? Choose four items of food and put them into your bowls. Once you've got the hang of moving food from one bowl to another, why don't you try eating it? Good luck!

Top tip!

Practice makes perfect, so don't get down-hearted if you don't become an overnight chopstick pro. Just remember, everyone has to start somewhere, even Chinese girls and boys.

Before you go...

What about creating your own Chinese banquet? What better way to practise eating with chopsticks than to eat a real Chinese meal together? Order a takeaway, go out to a restaurant or cook the food yourselves. At the back of the book you'll find recipes for a Chinese meal that should tickle your taste buds and give you some delicious practice in using chopsticks...

Chapter 4

When fingers work best

A note to the grown-ups

Cutlery has a place in our society, as do fast food and sticky fingers.

I am dead against *not* allowing children some leeway when it comes to how they eat their food. Personally, I wouldn't dream of eating a hamburger without a knife and fork, but I'm an adult, and getting my hands sticky and covered in layers of meat grease, mayo and tomato ketchup isn't something I revel in. However, my children do. They love it, they always have. And, depending on the circumstances, who am I to stop them?

What I have tried to do with my own children, as well as the children I have taught, is give them a sense of propriety.

One day, a lady brought her little girl to one of my classes. The lady was quite adamant that her daughter needed a crash course in manners. She told me she felt mortified by something her child had done, but couldn't possibly tell me exactly what it was. Well, we continued talking, and then it all came out.

Apparently she and her daughter had been out for lunch with Prince Andrew and his two daughters. All the children ordered hamburgers and were given knives and forks to use, but before the lady could stop her daughter, she had happily rolled her sleeves up, ignored the knife and fork, and picked her hamburger up with her hands. It was a hamburger, after all. Why shouldn't she use her fingers? That's what she'd do in a burger bar or her own home.

The lady had berated her daughter sternly for having no idea about manners, but I had to gently make the point that *the child had done nothing wrong*. She simply wasn't aware (because she hadn't been *made* aware) that if you're in a restaurant and you're given a knife and fork, it doesn't matter whether you're about to eat chicken nuggets, hamburger or pizza, you should use the knife and fork.

So the main aim of this chapter is to try to encourage your child to start thinking about what is appropriate behaviour, and to know when fingers get the thumbs-up.

We also talk through:

- Types of food that definitely only need fingers.

- Food that can be eaten with either fingers or cutlery.

There are shades of grey when it comes to some food, and that's where your guidance is necessary. Pizza, for example. If we're talking traditional Italian pizza with a thin crust and few ingredients, I'd say why not use your fingers? But if we're talking, thick crust, eight toppings and a pizza so bendy you can't even lift it off the plate, it stands to reason that a knife and fork would work better – especially in a restaurant, because no one wants to watch other people masticating their food with large stringy bits of mozzarella hanging from their mouths!

Other foods that we'll be talking about include finger sandwiches, croissants and pastries, cakes, hamburgers and other fast food, asparagus, shellfish, and cheese and biscuits.

Younger children might not be into things like asparagus or shellfish, so don't feel you have to focus on every food. The important thing is that your child begins to realise that the place where they're eating, and whether or not they have been served cutlery, are two factors that should influence their decision about how they're going to eat their food.

I've found it works quite well to work your way through the chapter before lunch or tea, so that you can then practise some of the lessons together on an actual meal.

As an example, for lunch you could both prepare two halves of a pizza. Keep one half light with few ingredients (so it's like a traditional pizza), and on the other half pile on a selection of toppings, really overdoing it, so your children can see how a knife and fork make more sense when the pizza is bendy and covered in toppings.

Or you could go for a traditional tea – sandwiches (using pastry shapers to make them look a bit more interesting), cup cakes, sausage rolls, cheese and crackers. You could also put out a tart or a slice of chocolate cake so your children can see why it's easier to use a spoon or fork rather than fingers when it comes to some teatime treats.

Top tip!

It's very unlikely your child will remember all the examples we discuss in this chapter. So every time you're eating out with your children, help them to think about how they're eating their food, remind them of what we've talked about, and encourage them to look around at what other people are doing. That way they'll learn how to work out what to do in all sorts of situations.

When fingers work best

Cutlery isn't always the best answer to eating food. Sometimes it actually makes more sense to use your fingers.

Top tip!

It's always important to wash your hands before you eat, but it's especially important before eating with your fingers. Just think where they've been!

Finger sandwiches

Sandwiches come in many different shapes and sizes, but finger sandwiches come in one size: finger-sized.

Original finger sandwiches are made by cutting off the crusts, then cutting through the two pieces of bread, one on top of the other, from top to bottom, into four equal pieces. They actually look like fingers. They're easy to pick up and they're bite-sized. As a result you only need your fingers to eat them. But they can be any shape, as long as they're small: round, triangular, square, star-shaped – anything.

If you're given a sandwich that is too big to eat, simply cut it into four triangles and then pick it up with your fingers. If the crusts are still on and you don't want to eat the crusts, don't eat them. Leave them neatly on the side of your plate.

Croissants, pastries and cakes

French pastries are light and delicate and can be torn with your fingers, and so can croissants and pains au chocolat.

Danish pastries and fruit tarts are made out of a thicker pastry and often contain almonds, fruits and custard. They are much stickier and really need a pastry fork. A pastry fork is not very heavy and it has a flat edge that makes it really easy to cut through thicker pastry. Pastry forks have to be held in your right hand so that the flat edge is facing down.

Little brownies and flapjacks are easy to eat with your fingers, but what about a thick, sticky slice of chocolate cake? You want it in your mouth, not stuck to your fingers, so it's better to use a fork or spoon.

My rule of thumb is, if a pastry or cake looks gooey, bendy or runny, use a spoon or fork, whatever is easiest for you.

Cup cakes

Little cakes in bun cases are great finger food for parties. Take the whole cake on to your plate, peel the edges of the paper case and flatten it on to the plate. Then it's easy to pick up the cake. If you pick up a cake with the paper still around it, it's really tricky to eat and you end up nibbling bits of paper. After you've finished, fold up the paper case and move it to the edge of your plate, ready to make room for the next one.

Fast food

I have to be honest and tell you that I really don't like eating fast food like hamburgers and chicken nuggets with my fingers, but that's me. If you do, then go for it! I don't think anything's wrong with using your fingers. But as a favour to whoever has to wash your clothes, and to the people you're sitting with, please use your napkin when your fingers get sticky.

Let's talk more about hamburgers. Do you think there's a difference between eating a hamburger at a barbecue and eating a hamburger in a restaurant? (I mean the sort of place where there are tablecloths laid on the tables and cutlery laid out for you.)

The answer is, yes, there is!

When you're in a restaurant, have you noticed that after you've told the waiter what you'd like to eat, the waiter comes back and lays out new cutlery in front of you? The cutlery laid for you and the cutlery laid out for your mum and dad will not necessarily be the same. For example, if your father's ordered fish, he'll be given a fish knife and fork. If your mother's ordered spaghetti bolognese, she'll be given a fork and spoon. And if you've ordered a hamburger, you'll be given a knife and fork.

The reason we get given different cutlery is because the *maître d'* (the head waiter) wants to make our lives easy for us, and give us the cutlery that suits the food we've ordered. Would you eat soup with a fork? No! Would you eat a cake with a butter knife? Of course not.

So if you get given a knife and fork by a waiter to eat your hamburger, you're meant to use them.

When a waiter or a friend's mother gives you cutlery, it's because they don't want you to stuff a hamburger in your mouth and get mayo all over your hands (and possibly their furniture). If your friend's mother thinks it's OK for you to eat with your fingers she'll tell you. When a *maître d'* orders the waiter to give you cutlery, he's saying to you, 'You know, this hamburger is the biggest, juiciest, most gooey hamburger you're ever going to eat, so here's a knife and fork to help you out.'

Believe me, if there were waiters in Burger King or your local fish and chip shop, they'd be doing the same thing. But there aren't, so in those places, fingers are fine.

Pizza

I think it's fine to eat pizza with your fingers if it's a thin crust with not much topping.

Cut a thin slice, and then it's much more manageable. Pick up the slice, take one mouthful and *then put the slice back down on your plate*. Only pick up the slice when you're ready to take another bite. That way, you don't get a mouth full of food, and the tomato and mozzarella stay where they should, on the pizza, not on your favourite dress or T-shirt.

However, if you've got a bendy, thick pizza that's covered in every possible topping, use a knife and fork, otherwise you might end up with more of your pizza on your face than in your tummy.

Top tip!

If you put your burger or pizza slice down in between bites, your hands won't get so greasy. If you want your hands to get sticky and greasy then go ahead, just remember to wash them before you get back into your parents' car!

Chicken drumsticks, lamb chops and spare ribs
Fingers are fine if the drumsticks and chops have been served as 'finger food', that is with a napkin and without a knife and fork. But if they're part of your Sunday lunch and they're covered in gravy and bits of mashed potato, I'd say use your knife and fork.

Top tip!

When you're using fingers, it's more difficult to gauge how much food you're actually putting in your mouth, so the best thing to do is this: even though you're bringing the food up to your mouth, don't put it <u>into</u> your mouth. Take a bite <u>out</u> of it. That way you'll never end up biting off more than you can chew! And there's nothing worse than having a mouth full of food that's so big you can't even chew it properly. It squidges out of your mouth, gives you jaw ache and if you're not careful, a nasty case of indigestion.

Asparagus

You always pick asparagus up with your fingers at the stalk end. The stalk of the asparagus is hard and acts a bit like a fork handle for us, which is why we don't really need the help of any cutlery. The dark green tip of the asparagus is the delicious part. The stalk can be quite tough so once it starts becoming more difficult to chew, leave the rest of the stalk and place it to the side of your plate. You can dip the tip into a melted butter or hollandaise sauce (yellow sauce made out of eggs and cream) or just eat it plain.

Ask for a finger bowl if you're not given one. Finger bowls are filled with slices of lemon and warm water, and you simply rub the tips of your fingers in the water when you've finished and then dry them with your napkin.

Prawns, lobster and crab

Your fingers are the best pieces of cutlery you can use for shell-fish. You may be given pointy little implements to help you get to some of the more difficult parts of shellfish like crabs and lobsters. If you feel unsure how to use the various bits, ask a grown-up to show you. Prawns are one of my favourites! If you're given unshelled prawns, head and tail them first and then run your thumbs down the underbelly of the prawn, gently pushing the shell apart. Think of it as unbuttoning the prawn's jacket. Once the shell is removed, remove any eggs or the grey strip that you can often see on the back of the prawn. Put all the shells and leftover pieces on the side plate if you haven't been given an extra plate.

Oysters

Just as the stalk of the asparagus acts like a fork handle, the shell of the oyster acts like a spoon.

You are normally given a choice of sauces to put on your oysters – a squeeze of lemon, shallots in red wine vinegar, or Tabasco, which is quite spicy. Hold the shell open, make sure the flesh of the oyster is detached from the shell by using your oyster fork, and then pour the oyster into your mouth.

If you don't like the look of oysters and somebody asks you to try one, never feel you have to! It's perfectly OK to say, 'no, thank you'. (By the way, they don't taste of much other than sea-water, but a lot of people find them delicious.)

Mussels and clams

Like oysters, you can use the shell of a mussel or a clam like a spoon. This is particularly handy when you're eating a soup-based dish like *moules marinière*. Mussel and clam shells make great pincers, so the trick is to use one shell to pull out the other mussels and clams from their shells. By the way, if you see a mussel or clam and it looks more closed than open, don't eat it. The reason they're not open is because they've gone off.

Cheese and crackers

If a cheese knife hasn't been laid on to the table, use the same knife you used to cut the cheese to position the cheese on your cracker – it's less messy than using fingers. Then lift the cracker to your mouth with your fingers. Crackers are dry and, like biscuits, they are not meant for cutlery. (If you try cutting a cracker in half with a fork, you'll see why!)

The mix and match game!

Knives, forks, fingers or spoons? Match the cutlery (or the fingers) to the dishes pictured below. This covers some food and cutlery we've talked about in the last two chapters so if you're not sure, have a look at the previous pages.

fish

hamburger on laid table

asparagus

hamburger in carton

bread roll

slice of chocolate cake   chicken nuggets

Answers:

Fish – a fish knife and fork will help you take the skin off the fish and separate the meat from the bones. Hamburger on a plate – well, although it's a hamburger, I'd say a knife and fork. You'll make a real mess of the tablecloth otherwise! Asparagus – fingers work best. Hamburger in a carton – well, you could either use your fingers or a knife and fork. A bread roll – why not use your fingers? Chocolate cake – you could use either a fork or a spoon. Chicken nuggets – you can use your fingers, but please use a napkin.

Top tip!

If you're ever out or at someone's house and you feel unsure as to whether you should be using cutlery or your fingers, the easiest rule of thumb is: <u>if you're given cutlery to use, there's a good reason to use it.</u>

Before you go...

Tell each other three things you've learnt from reading this chapter.

Chapter 5

Sharing a meal with other people

A note to the grown-ups

As adults, we know instinctively that it's impolite to spit out our food or eat with our mouths open. However, our children have not yet been exposed to the number or variety of social situations we have. We are not always going to be standing at our children's shoulders, so in teaching them what is appropriate behaviour, part of our job is to expose them to as many different situations as possible so they can start to learn how to edit their own behaviour depending on who they're with and what environment they're in. That way we can ensure that when our children grow up, they won't be the person shovelling peas into their mouth or dripping gravy juice down their chin that everyone else is pretending not to look at.

And our hope is that they will then see for themselves that the decision they make about the *way* they eat isn't just based on them making life easier for themselves. It is also to do with consideration and respect for others.

I've seen a well-known actor hosting a dinner party for eight people ignore the knife and fork in front of him and smugly pick up a gravy-soaked chicken leg and start eating it, head down, nose to the plate, ignoring the rest of his guests (but with the odd sideways glance to check they were looking at him). He thought he was being clever. 'Hey! I've got money! I'm paying for this suite, I'm paying for this dinner, so I can do what I want! And that goes for how I eat my chicken legs!' He wasn't thinking about the people on either side of him who now had no one to talk to (how can you talk to someone if their head is hanging over a plate?). He wasn't thinking about how, every time he did look up, it wasn't a pretty sight to see the grease and gravy smeared all over his face. In short, the only person he was really thinking about was himself.

It upsets me when I see a person not respecting the other people they are sharing a meal with. I don't care whether they're sitting at a kitchen table in a council house, in the banqueting room of a palace or at the trendiest restaurant in London. Sharing a meal with anyone is a time to show consideration, and this is a fundamental lesson that I try to instil during my classes.

When I'm talking to children about not eating with their mouths open, or not getting down from the table while other people are still eating, I don't just say, 'Don't do it, it's not nice.' I explain to them – and their parents – how disrespectful it is to the other people around the table.

Sometimes the best way to get a lesson across is to demonstrate, as a regular guest at the Lanesborough once did.

A couple of years ago I was lucky enough to look after a wonderful lady who is a rock star. She had been a guest of the hotel before and her children were known to be very well behaved. But during this particular lunch, which she had ordered to be served in her suite, they were acting up. Her son was sitting at the table, stuffing pizza in his mouth and then squidging it out between the gaps where his milk teeth had fallen out. His sister was loving the show and trying to copy him.

Their mother asked them to stop several times, but they ignored her.

As quick as a flash, she grabbed a huge piece of pizza, rammed it all into her mouth and then started singing. Bits of pizza went flying and hit her children. She leant over the table and, opening her mouth wide, showed both of them what she was eating while she sang. To a chorus of 'gross!' and cries of 'stop!' she coolly shut her mouth, apologised to me for the mess, sat back down and said, 'Do that again and next time it'll be opera.'

The little boy and girl ate the rest of their lunch in perfect peace and harmony.

To help a child understand why he should bother to behave in a considerate manner, we have to be able to show them *why* we bother – and that *we* bother. It might seem like an uphill struggle at times – believe me, I've been there! Despite all my experience teaching children manners, my own children, all five of them, have at times driven me bananas – but the one thing to keep in mind is that through your perseverance and patience, you're giving your child a great gift: *an awareness of how to behave in a considerate way*.

In this chapter we talk through:

- Basic table manners, so your child knows what to do when you're not there.

- What your child can expect when they eat at a friend's house, or in a restaurant.

- Questions and answers on mealtime quandaries, from the child's point of view, e.g. if you drop a piece of cutlery at someone's house, if you don't like the food you're being offered, or if you're bored.

- How to eat some of the more tricky foods we eat, e.g. spaghetti, fish.

As this is quite a long chapter, if your child is in the younger age bracket, I'd stop after 'table manners you can take anywhere', to make sure he or she has a chance to take everything on board.

Before I go, here's a note on something that's really close to my heart…

Why TV dinners are bad news

I believe sharing a meal at the table with your child or children is one of the most important and giving things you can do as a parent. It's not just about eating; it's also about talking, and laughing, and arguing. It means that, for thirty minutes or so, you are both sharing a slice of life. (As my children have hit their teens, mealtimes are now often the only time I get to find out what's going on in their lives.)

Children are sponges for information. They watch you, they listen to what you say. You are their role model for life. If *you* think it's OK not to say please and thank you, then so will your children. If *you* think it's OK to use only a fork and your fingers to eat your meal, so will your children.

You are probably full of wonderful ideas about how you'd like to bring your children up and what you'd like to teach them, but the question is, how do you communicate it all to them? Well, there's no quick fix. Children aren't computers that you insert a new piece of software into and then – whizz! – all the information's there. It's a drip, drip campaign. Slowly, day by day, they soak it up both consciously and subconsciously. And a great place to start (and continue) this process is at the table.

I've got nothing against the occasional TV dinner, just as long as they don't happen all the time. But you know the stereotype of the large Italian family having lunch together, conversations overlapping, family members gesticulating wildly as they laugh and argue their way through life? And the image of the English 2.4 family stooped over their trays, illuminated by the glow of the TV, tucking into their food and not saying a word to each other? I know which image I warm to.

In this country there seems to be a move away from families sitting down together, which concerns me so much that I feel I have to speak out. OK, sitting in front of the TV eating your supper is relaxing. You switch off from work and escape from your day-to-day worries in a TV drama. The problem is that, when you do this, you're also inadvertently switching off from the people who are sitting in the room with you.

I really recommend trying to sit down at the table to eat together as a family, even if it's only one lunch and one evening a week. If you find it difficult to fit it into your life, plan the date you're going to do it, so you and your partner can both make arrangements to be home earlier. And then, with the TV switched off and the conversation started, see what soap story unfurls around your own kitchen table. At the same time you can keep an eye on how your children's manners are developing, what they still need to learn, and whether or not they're learning the right cues from you.

Props

You will need:
2 biscuits, 2 dry crackers, or two packets of crisps, and you should be seated side by side at the table where you eat your meals.

In the first section, 'Table manners you can take anywhere', the table has to be laid, but it might be good practice for your child to have a go at doing it instead of you. Tell them what you're going to be eating and see if they can work out what cutlery they need to lay and where.

When we talk through some of the more tricky foods children come across, like spaghetti, oranges, noodle soup and fish, it's a good idea to have examples of these foods to hand, so you can both practise eating them the 'easy way'.

A word on age expectations:

- On the whole, I don't think children under the age of eight years should be expected to sit at a table for more than one hour.

- If you're going to a restaurant or a friend's house and your children are under ten years of age, let them bring along some colouring books, puzzles or their favourite book. Or perhaps some blank paper and pens so they can draw or play hangman or similar games.

- Once children are ten or older, they should be able to sit at the table with you for the duration of the meal, without games or props.

Things worth thinking about

- If your child starts complaining about being bored early on during the meal, before you tell them off, pause and think: 'Am I involving them in the conversation?' You'd get bored if you were sitting at a table and two other people were talking over your head about a subject that meant nothing to you.

- If you're taking your child along to your friend's house and you're going to be chatting, let them bring along a Game Boy, a book or a favourite toy. It's not much fun for them otherwise.
- If you want to take your children out for a meal, go to a restaurant that is child-friendly. Sadly, there are some restaurants that still think children should be neither seen nor heard, and you'll just get stressed if you go to one of these. I find Italian and Chinese restaurants are normally

good – their culture is child-friendly and children generally like their food. As a parent, you want to relax and get good vibes from the staff around you, not raised eyebrows if, in a moment of excitement, your child's voice goes up one decibel.

- Make sure that the restaurant you take them to is not slow for service. If the children you are with are under eight years old, you don't want to waste half an hour of their fidget-free time waiting for their food.

Sharing a meal with other people

It doesn't bother me how you eat when you're by yourself. You can lick the yoghurt out of the yoghurt pot, skim your fingers around the inside of your pudding bowl, dunk biscuits into your favourite drink, or soak up the gravy from your plate with a piece of bread! Really, it doesn't bother me, because I'll never have to look at you doing it, and neither will anyone else.

Let's be honest, sometimes it's a real bother to use your knife and fork, isn't it? When you're tired or hungry, all you want to do is pick up that tasty-looking knot of spaghetti with your fingers, lift up that huge chicken leg that's covered with gravy from your plate, and push it all in your mouth in one go.

And sometimes you don't want to use your knife and fork because you're having too much fun. Let's say you're having tea at a friend's house, and both of you get a bit carried away. You start blowing bubbles in your drink, throwing pieces of bread at each other and squidging food between your teeth. And then you start having a food fight…

Have you ever thought about what happens to the food once you've flicked it, thrown it or squished it? Maybe you don't think there's anything wrong in doing any of the above?

Well, see what you think of what happened to Harry and Angelica.

Harry and Angelica were invited to their friend Percy's house for tea, and Percy's mum cooked them a delicious cottage pie. Angelica, Harry and Percy decided it would be fun to have a food fight with it. They had a brilliant time, but the same can't be said for Percy's mum. She's still trying to get the gravy stains off her walls, and Percy has been told that, no matter how much he likes Angelica and Harry, he can't invite them back to the house again, which is a pity, because Angelica and Harry used to love going over to his house, and his mum was always very kind to them and always gave them little treats when they visited.

What do you think about what Harry, Angelica and Percy did? What do you think they are thinking now?

Now tell me what you think of what Robbie got up to.

The other Saturday, Jen, Robbie and Mai went to the cinema. Robbie quite likes Mai. In fact he's got a bit of a crush on her, so he's always keen to impress her. After the cinema they went for a pizza. Their pizzas took ages to come, and Robbie was starving by the time his finally arrived. So starving, in fact, that he gobbled his up without even checking to see if the girls had got theirs (they hadn't). He ate the whole pizza in three minutes flat – a fact he was quite proud of until he realised that he should have offered some of his pizza to Mai and Jen, who had to wait another ten minutes for theirs to arrive.

What do you think Mai thinks of Robbie now?

The fact is, it matters how we eat and how we behave when we're sharing a meal with other people, especially when we're eating at someone else's house, because if we don't behave in a kind and caring way, they'll think we don't like them enough to bother.

I'll let you in on a secret. Sometimes grown-ups feel the same way you do.

Sometimes we want to leave the table while people are still eating.

We want to burp loudly if we've got indigestion.

We want to ignore someone talking to us because we're not very interested in what they're talking about.

But we don't.

Why?

Because we know people have feelings, grown-ups and children alike, and none of us likes having our feelings hurt.

If you spit out a piece of cake that your sister's baked, you'll hurt her feelings.

If you ignore a boy or girl who's talking to you at school, you're hurting their feelings.

If a friend's mother invites you for tea and you tell her, 'I don't like this pie, it's horrible,' you're hurting her feelings.

Now that doesn't mean you have to eat food that you really don't like (more about this later...) but it does mean that when you're with other people, it's always a good idea to think before you act!

Top tip!

When you're about to say or do something and you're not sure it's OK, ask yourself: how would I feel if someone did or said this to me? Think first!

Do you remember when we talked about respecting other people's feelings in Chapter 1? Well, when you're sharing a meal with other people, it's a good time to practise all those ways of being considerate to other people, like saying 'please' and 'thank you' and 'excuse me'.

Now, let's have a look at other things you can do...

Talking with your mouth full

Imagine you're sitting next to *you* at the dinner table.

Would you want to see you eating with your mouth open? If you're not sure of the answer – and even if you are – why don't you and your mum or dad do the following experiment together?

Experiment!

You will need:

2 crackers, 2 biscuits, or a packet of crisps each and 2 glasses of water.

Take some big bites out of your cracker or a generous handful of crisps and start chewing! Face each other and begin to chew with your mouths open. Wide open. Now take a drink of water. Chew, chew, chew! And put some more crisps into your mouth.

What does your mum or dad look like? Do you like looking at the inside of their mouth?

Go and have a look in a mirror. What do you look like?

Now take some more bites and try to start talking to each other while you're chewing. Is it easy? What's happening to all the bits of crisps and crackers?

It's not a pretty sight, is it?

The fact is, no one likes looking into someone else's mouth, especially when it's full of mushed-up food!

Top tip!

If someone asks you a question and you're in the middle of eating something, simply point to your mouth and nod your head so they realise you're eating. You can answer them at your own leisure once you've swallowed your food.

Table manners

'Table manners' sound boring, but in fact they're really useful. They help you out of tricky situations and they help you stay relaxed and happy when you're eating with people.

I once watched a grown-up in our hotel restaurant pick up a finger bowl, and, because he was too embarrassed to ask what it was there for, he drank it, thinking it was a special drink.

I've seen children in a restaurant accidentally knock their food on to the floor and then not know whether to pick it up or not.

Or what if you go to a friend's house and then get served with a dish of food that contains some of your least favourite vegetables? Do you eat it or not?

There are all sorts of questions and confusions that could arise – but do not despair! Help is at hand.

The list of basic table manners below will help you feel more comfortable and relaxed when you're dining without your parents, at someone else's house, or in a restaurant. They're simple and easy to follow.

Table manners you can take anywhere

Game

Stand up and pretend you're about to sit down for a meal at a friend's house. One of you pretend to be the host or hostess, and the other the guest.

Before you start, please lay the table for two people. You need: 2 large knives, 2 large forks, 2 plates and 2 napkins.

T is for Table.

Guest: Wait to be invited to sit at the table. The host or hostess (either your friend's parent or your friend) will show you where to sit.

Host/Hostess: Show your guest where they should sit down. Where are you going to sit?

A is for Asking.

Guest: Are you too low at the table to eat comfortably? If you are, ask the host for a cushion. There's nothing wrong in asking if you ask nicely. 'Please may I…' is always a good opener.

Host/Hostess: Do you need a cushion? Does your guest have everything they need?

B is for Beginning to eat.

You both should now be sitting down. Once you're comfortable, sit up straight, with your legs in front of you, under the table, and keep your elbows off the table. When you put your elbows on the table, you take up space needed for your plate and cutlery, and you generally end up putting your elbows in some food, so it's better to keep them at your side.

When everyone has sat down, pick up your napkin. If you're under eight years old you can either tuck your napkin into your shirt or the neck of your dress or if you're over eight or you prefer, unfold your napkin and place it over your lap.

Guest: Only start to eat when everyone has been served their food, and the host or hostess has picked up their cutlery or invited you to start.

L is for Laughing and enjoying yourself.

The whole idea behind sharing a meal with other people is to enjoy their company. If you're sitting having a family meal at home, really listen to what the other members of your family are talking about. You never know, they might be more interesting than you think they are. And if you're eating in a restaurant or a friend's house, it's a great opportunity to find out about other people.

Sometimes talking to people you don't know that well can be embarrassing, especially if you're a bit shy. That's when it's a good idea to ask questions. People love answering questions, especially when they're about themselves. It's also a good way to get people talking.

Guest and host: Can you think of three questions you could ask each other now?

Top tip!

Questions for grown-ups can be about their favourite holidays, hobbies, books or movies. Questions for children can be about holidays, school, books or movies.

E is for Eating.

Well, as we've discovered, people don't look their best if they don't eat properly. Nobody wants to see into another person's mouth, especially if it's full of mushed-up food! To make life easy for yourself, take bite-size pieces of food as they are easier to chew.

And remember, it's better to bring your fork to your mouth rather than lowering your head to your fork, because the closer your head gets to your plate, the more likely it is that you might get your hair covered in sauce and food. (Also, it's pretty boring looking at a plate. It's much more fun to watch what's going on around you.)

Quick quiz

Can you remember what the letters of **TABLE** stand for? Shut the book!

Escape routes from tricky situations

Below are the questions I've been asked most frequently about table manners. I hope you find the answers useful.

- *If you don't know which cutlery to use…*
  If you're faced with lots of cutlery, remember the saying:

  Forks and spoons and knives a spin
  Always work from outside in!

  And if in doubt, ask.

  (Have a look at Chapter 2 if you want to remind yourself about the different bits of cutlery.)

- *If you can't reach some food on the table…*
  Don't try to! Leaning over people to get a dish isn't a great idea. If they were eating, you could accidentally push their fork into their mouth, and if you were to stretch over the table, you would very likely end up spilling or knocking over other food that's in the way. To solve this problem, simply ask the person who is sitting closest to the dish if they would mind passing you the potatoes or sausages, whatever

it is you'd like. If the person is more than an arm's length away, they will pass the dish to someone closer to you who can then hand it over to you.

- *If you want seconds…*
  Normally you will be offered a little more if there's any left. If you're not offered any, it probably means it's all gone. If this is the end of the meal and you are still hungry … wait until you get home.

- *If you burp, fart, sneeze or cough…*
  If you burp or cough, cover your mouth with your hand first. If you're going to sneeze, cover your mouth and nose and turn your head slightly away from the table. If you don't have a handkerchief, *in emergency situations only*, use your napkin. Remember, everybody burps, everybody farts, even the Queen! Simply say 'Excuse me' and leave it at that.

Top tip!

You never know when you're going to sneeze, so it's always worth having a tissue or handkerchief handy.

- *If someone else burps or farts…*
  Now, I know we all laugh about these things, but really, the thing you *must not* do in situations like these is make a fuss about it. Remember when we were talking about hurting people's feelings? Well, how would you like it if you farted and someone drew attention to it? You'd feel embarrassed, wouldn't you? So, as tempting as it might be to laugh and giggle about it, *ignore it*!

- *If you drop your cutlery or some food on to the floor...*
  If you're out at a restaurant, draw the waiter's attention to
  the bit of food or piece of cutlery that has fallen on to the
  floor. As he's the one who has to kneel down to pick it up, a
  little smile or a quick apology would be nice. The waiter will
  then give you a clean piece of cutlery.

  Equally, if you're at a friend's house, tell a grown-up
  what's happened (again, with a quick apology), and they'll
  be happy to help you. If you've dropped some food, you
  could ask for a dustpan and brush. Offering to help is a
  good thing to do.

- *If you don't like the food you're being offered...*
  You don't have to tell everyone or make a big fuss. A simple 'no thank you' is as easy to say as 'I don't like that', and much less hurtful. Or, if you've been given it anyway, it's perfectly polite to leave food on your plate – there's no rule that says you have to eat *everything*.

  Having said that, it's fine to say, 'no thank you' to a couple of things, but you can't say 'no thank you' to everything. If you look hard enough, you can always find something on the table or the plate that you can eat.

Top tip!

If you are given a meal and you don't like something that's been put on your plate – like Brussels sprouts or carrots – don't make a fuss. It's easier to simply move the bits of the meal you don't like around your plate, and leave them at the side.

- *If you need to go to the toilet...*
  Say 'Excuse me' to the people sitting next to you. Get up from the table and leave your napkin on your chair. If you don't know where the toilet is, ask one of the people you're sitting next to for directions.

- *If you get bored...*
  Well, ask yourself if you could be making more of an effort. It's easy to get bored if you sit there in silence and don't try to join in. Why not try asking people questions and really listening to what they're talking about?

  However, if the people around you are not doing a great

job at involving you in their conversation (grown-ups can do this, though it's not intentional), nothing's wrong in gently reminding them that you're there, and that finances or insurance are not things you know a lot about!

Top tip!

Don't make decisions too quickly about whether people are interesting or not. Often they're shy, and if you bother to make the effort and get things going with a few questions, you can end up really enjoying their company.

- *If you get the hiccups...*
  You were eating too quickly – hiccups are your body's way of saying, 'Hey, slow down!' Simply say 'Excuse me' and try taking some sips from a glass of water. They will go away – eventually – so don't worry.

- *If you want to leave the table while people are still eating...*
  Well, you can't. Because it's rude. How would you like it if you were left at the table sitting there by yourself because nobody could be bothered to wait for you? When you sit down at the table with other people, you must leave the table only when everyone is ready to leave. And I don't care how fidgety you are.

  Of course, if everyone's finished eating dessert, you can always ask the grown-up in charge, 'Please may I get down from the table?'

- *When you're at someone else's house...*

  If you're having a meal at a friend's house and your parents aren't around to guide you, take your cue from your friend's parents and your friend. Sit at the table when your friend sits, only leave the table when your friend leaves. Go with the flow. Copy what they do. Let your friend take control and do all the asking. After all, you don't know what his or her family rules are, so it's better to take a back seat and watch and wait.

  However, if you've finished your drink and you're still thirsty and you've waited to be offered another one but no one has seen, it's completely OK to ask for one. The opener, 'Excuse me. Please may I...' goes down a treat with people.

Top tip!

If you're unsure about anything, like where the toilet is, or what the ingredients are in a dish of food, <u>ask, ask, ask!</u> Remember, just as long as you ask nicely, nobody minds.

Tricky food

Some food is easy to eat, some isn't, whether you're a grown-up or a child. Oranges squirt juice into your eye, strings of spaghetti won't go into your mouth, peas run away from you, noodles are so slippery you can never fish them out of your soup...

Believe me, it's as bad for grown-ups as it is for you!

But here are a few tips on how to eat some particularly

tricky examples, so that you enjoy your food and your food ends up where it should: in your mouth, not on the tablecloth.

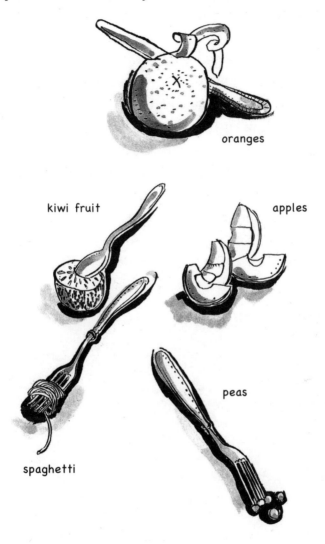

oranges

kiwi fruit

apples

peas

spaghetti

Pasta ribbons and spaghetti
Best cutlery to use: a spoon and fork.

First of all, for those of you who are younger, before you even begin tucking into your delicious bowl of spaghetti bolognese, ask a grown-up to cut through the pasta so it's easier to handle. Then, with your napkin tucked into your top, or covering your lap, pick up the fork with your right hand and the spoon with your left hand (or swap them round if you're left-handed).

Now dig into the pile of spaghetti with your fork, roll your fork into your spoon and twist it. Beware of overtwisting! You don't want a huge roll of spaghetti otherwise it won't be able to go into your mouth.

If you do end up with too much, simply unravel the spaghetti back on to the spoon, shake a bit off your fork and start again. It's quite normal to sometimes end up with a stray piece of spaghetti dangling out of your mouth. Simply nibble it and, using your fork, guide it back on to your plate.

It takes a while to get good at spaghetti, so why not cook up your favourite pasta dish for lunch or dinner so you can practise?

Noodles and noodle soup

Best cutlery to use: a soup spoon.

You can eat plain noodles exactly as you would eat spaghetti. If the noodles are wet and in a soup, it's not a good idea to try and suck the noodles up into your mouth. All that happens is that you end up being slapped in the face by out-of-control wet noodles! The trick is to use the edge of the spoon to cut the noodles into bite-size lengths while they're still in the soup, then they'll fit easily onto your spoon.

Fish

Best cutlery to use: a fish knife and fork (see page 42 to see what a fish knife looks like).

The easiest way to remove the skin of a cooked fish is to take your fork and, with the help of your knife, start rolling the skin off the fish on to your fork. You can then leave the skin on the side of your plate. Used horizontally, the flat fish knife is great for skimming the flesh of the fish off the bone. However, remember you always have the choice to ask for your fish off the bone, or, if you're stuck, ask a grown-up to help you.

Peas

Best cutlery to use: a knife and fork.

If you're under ten years old, don't worry about eating peas the adult way. Just rest the back of your fork on your plate and, using your knife, guide the peas on to your fork as if it were a spoon. Try not to put too many peas on your fork as they'll be difficult to balance.

If you're over ten years old, you'll be able to manage eating peas the adult way. So, with your fork prongs facing down, stick the peas on to the prongs of your fork using your knife, and push them up against the back of the fork to secure them (see below).

The trick is to use your knife and fork to 'herd' together a pile of peas on your plate as they are then easier to pick up.

Fruit

Best cutlery to use: a knife and a fork.

It's fine to eat fruit with your fingers, but if you're not careful, you can end up with more of the fruit on you than in your mouth. The techniques below are great for making sure you don't get covered in juice and don't get any pips in your mouth either.

If you're under ten years old, let an adult do the cutting.

Apples

Cut the apple in half with your knife, then into quarters. Take the middle, hard bit of each slice of apple and run your knife down it, in a scooping action, not going very deep. By doing this you can get rid of the hard, pipped core. Slice the quarters into bite-size slices, as and when you feel like it.

Oranges

Cut a thin piece off the bottom and top of the orange so the orange can sit flat on your plate. Then, slice the rind and pith away from the orange, cutting down from top to bottom. When the rind has gone, you can turn the orange on to its side and cut slices off as and when required. Pop them into your mouth with the fork. This is a great way to keep the juice of the orange in the orange and not sprayed on to your clothes. Have a practice at home.

Manners from heaven

Kiwi fruit

Cut the fruit in half across its middle. Now, holding one half of the kiwi fruit down on your plate, you can scoop the flesh out of the 'pot' of the kiwi fruit with a teaspoon.

If you're over ten, you can use the same cutting technique we used for cutting the orange instead, if you like: cut the skin off and then slice it as you want it.

Before you go...

Choose your favourite fruits from the above list, grab yourself a plate and a small knife and fork, and, with the help of an adult, have a go at cutting them up the grown-up way.

Tell each other three things that you have each learnt from this chapter.

Chapter 6

Party time! – Invitations

A note to the grown-ups

In the twenty-first century, invitations have taken on a more important sociological role than they ever had before. It wasn't that long ago that the 'village community' worked perfectly effectively as a communications network. People lived next to each other's parents and grandparents, there was a central meeting place – the village/church hall or pub – and children just happened to bump into each other in the park or could easily walk over to each other's houses to ask if 'Angelica can come out to play'. This has now mutated into a far more complex set-up. Nowadays, you won't always know the people living next to you. You won't necessarily know all the names of your children's friends' parents from school. And why should you? You probably only see some of them for a cursory nod on Parents' Evening or a brief chat when you're picking your children up from a party.

Children's invitations have become, sometimes, the only route for children to develop friendships outside school, so they have to be nurtured.

One of the most important lessons I teach the children in my classes is that, whether an invitation is written or spoken, it should be treated with respect and consideration. I tell them they should:

- Always reply to an invitation, as soon as possible.

- Never cancel an invitation, once accepted, in favour of a better one. Personally I find people who do this incredibly rude. I don't care how fantastic the second invitation is, I don't care whether it's from the Queen herself; once you've accepted an invitation, you should always go.

- Never change their mind about accepting or refusing an invitation. Once they've replied, that's it.

Until your children are well into their teens, you will play a pivotal role in enabling them to reply to invitations and to turn up to the party on the right day, dressed correctly, at the right time, in the right place. This is a huge responsibility, but it will help you a lot if your child is aware of at least the basics of good manners when it comes to sending out and receiving invitations. They will then be more amenable to helping you leave the house on time, remember the present, and generally (in my experience) take on a bit more responsibility.

In this chapter I take you and your child through:

- Written invitations – information that you *need* to put on an invitation.

- Information that you may want to put on an invitation.

Clearly younger children will be dependent on you to write the invitations and to reply on their behalf, but it's still a great idea to get them involved. The sooner they start seeing how this particular social ritual works, the quicker they'll learn.

It's a good idea to go through this chapter when your child has either received an invitation or needs to send one off, as it makes everything we talk about more relevant and sticks in their mind better.

Sending out invitations

- If your child doesn't want to invite someone to their party, you shouldn't immediately go along with their wish. Children make friends and fall out with them as quickly as the weather changes (British weather, that is!). Ask yourself what the form is at your child's school – do all the children in their class get invited to each other's birthday parties? Do children just select a small group? This situation changes as children grow up (they tend to ask fewer and fewer), but you need to do your own research to gauge what the right thing to do is, for your child, at this moment in time.

- You should never let your child consider 'disinviting' someone to their party. No matter how big they think the argument with their friend has been, once an invitation has been given, it is incredibly rude to rescind it. The only time this has ever happened in my experience was when the birthday boy or girl was sick.

- Send out invitations between three and four weeks before the date of a party.

- If it's a more casual invitation – perhaps an invitation to tea – I'd say call the child's parent a week or two before the date you've got in mind.

- If you like the mother of a child, but your child has made it very clear she or he doesn't warm to *their* child, don't try and force them into a play-date. It's not much fun for either child to be forced into playing with each other simply to fit in with your social diary.

Replying to invitations

- As soon as your child hands over an invitation, check the family diary and reply *immediately*. Leaving it a couple of days makes it more likely you'll forget to reply.

- If the invitation is spoken, immediately write down the details in the family diary on the relevant day. Too often I have depended on my memory, then the cat's been sick or my son has run out of petrol on the A3, and whizz! It's like pressing the delete button on my mental computer, and the details disappear into the ether.

• Once you've replied, put a tick (acceptance) or a cross (declined) on the invitation. Keep all the invitations plus any maps or additional information your child receives in one place – perhaps stuck on a family memo board – so the information's to hand if anyone needs to get hold of it.

• When you write or call to accept an invitation on your child's behalf, tell the host/hostess then and there if your child has any specific dietary or medical requirements. It is your responsibility to pass this information on. And if you are incredibly worried – perhaps your child is diabetic or has a severe nut allergy – ask if they mind if you remain at the party. Believe me, they won't. There is only so much responsibility a parent can take for people's children, especially when there is a marauding, overexcited horde of them to take care of!

• Having said that, obviously you don't want to be overspecific – there's no need to give a whole list of foods that your child 'likes and quite likes'. After all, part of the point of your child going to other people's

Becky's gluten free and I'm still keeping her away from acid fruit – her bowel movements get too loose, alkaline's fine but no fruit after six pm and no wheat, definitely no non-organic meat, but.....................

Are you sure you don't want Jessica to come and play instead?

houses is for them to realise that things can be done differently and that not all people are the same.

Props

Have some old invitations handy so your child can see different examples of invitations, and some blank paper and coloured pens or pencils so you can both have a go at designing your own.

Top tip!

Please remember that there is no such thing as being fashionably late when it comes to children's parties. No parent likes to feel like their house is being used as a day-care centre, so if the invitation has a drop-off and pick-up time on it, make sure you stick to them.

Party time! – Invitations

I love receiving invitations, and I love sending them out. The huge excitement you feel when you write a date in your diary for a party you've accepted is one thing you never grow out of, thank goodness. And of course, when it's your own party you have the excitement of the run-up to the whole thing. What games are you going to play? What are you going to eat?

Look at the illustration. It's an invitation to Jennifer's birthday party – she designed it herself.

CONGRATULATIONS!

You have been invited to Jen's birthday party!

Where should I go?
The Coronet Cinema. 2.30 p.m. prompt.

Then how about a pizza?
Pizza Express, Old Street 4.30 p.m.

What should I wear? **Boho cool!**
The party's over at 6.30 p.m.

RSVP by 2nd October:
✉ Email: Susie_Johnson@virgin.com.uk
or
☎ ring 0191 111 2233

Map attached.
Pizza Express's number is 0191 444 5566

If you're the host or the hostess, it's a good idea to send out invitations for your party between three and four weeks before the date, as this gives the parents of your friends time to plan and rearrange things if necessary.

Look at the information Jennifer's put on her invitation. Can you spot the one really important piece of information that she hasn't mentioned?

Sending out an invitation

Important facts that you must tell people are:

The date: Very important!

The time: You need to say what time the party is going to start, and it's usually a good idea to give a time for the party to finish.

Jennifer has invited some friends to the cinema and then pizza. If her friends don't turn up at 2.30 p.m. exactly they'll miss the film which is why she's put 'prompt' next to the time. That way, her friends' parents will know that they have to get their children to the cinema exactly at that time.

The place: If you're having your party somewhere other than your home and the place is not very well known, it's a great idea to attach a map. You could print off a local map from the internet, or you could ask the location where you're hold-ing the party if they have one. Sometimes a pointer is enough, like 'under the bridge, opposite the town hall'. Otherwise, a freehand map is a good idea, showing all the landmarks your friends and their parents are familiar with.

Top tip!

If you're going to a place like a restaurant or an ice-skating rink, it's worth putting the telephone number of the place down on the invitation just in case people get lost and need some more directions on the day.

Who to reply to: Even though your friends will tell you whether they can come to your party or not, their parents must *always reply* too, as they are in control of the family diary. Put your mother's or father's first name on the invitation next to the telephone number or e-mail address, just in case your friends' parents don't know their names.

How to reply: In this day and age, I don't think a hand-written reply is the only 'proper' way to reply. We have other ways to communicate that are faster and just as effective – email address, telephone number, text. All you want to know is *whether your friends can make it or not*. Ask your parents how they would like your friends' parents to respond, and then give your guests two options on how to reply. That way they have no excuse for not getting back to you quickly.

Top tip!

There's a shorthand for writing 'how to reply' that everyone uses: R.S.V.P. It's an abbreviation of the French 'Répondez, s'il vous plaît' (reply, please). Put it in the bottom left-hand corner of the invitation with the details about how to reply.

Date to reply by: Unfortunately some children and their parents are very lazy about replying to invitations. I don't see anything wrong with putting a 'reply by' date on your invitation – this will help you receive all your replies on time. Remember, your parents will need to know the final number of guests so they can buy the right amount of food and party treats, or book the right-sized table, so why should they be inconvenienced by ill-mannered grown-ups?

Dress: If you've agreed with your parents that you'd like a themed or fancy-dress party, it's really important you tell your guests this in their invitation. Equally, if you're going to be out-side doing some sport, for example, your friends need to know what they should bring – tennis shoes, trainers, or warm clothes for ice-skating, for instance.

P. S. Jennifer forgot to mention the date. Oops!

What should your invitation be written on?

It's up to you! In the olden days people used to like writing invitations on thick card, not paper. I don't think it really mat-ters what you write your invitations on or how you do them. The more fun you have creating them, the better. You can draw your own, buy ready-made ones, or email all the details to your friends. Just as long as the *important facts* are written down, it's really up to you.

Different invitations

Guess what? Auntie Sarah's getting married!

Below are a couple of different examples of invitations to her wedding for you to look at. As you can see, they might look very different from each other, but if you look closely, you'll see they all in fact carry the same information. Which invitation looks the most formal? Which looks the most fun? Which one do you think she should choose to send out?

> *Mr and Mrs Derek Geddes*
>
> *request the pleasure of your company
> at the wedding of their daughter*
>
> *Sarah Hutchinson to
> Lord Ponsibly Bigbottom at
> All Saints Church, Whitburn*
>
> *On 25 August 2006, 4 p.m.
> Dinner and dancing: 6 p.m.
> Dress: Black tie
> Carriages: Midnight
> R.S.V.P. by 1 August*

When the party finishes. This is from the olden days, before cars, when people got around by horse-drawn carriage. It sounds nicer than 'cars'.

The R.S.V.P. date is three weeks before the actual date of the wedding because invitations to important social events like weddings and big parties like balls are sent out six weeks before the date of the event.

Sarah's getting married!

Mr and Mrs Derek Geddes
are delighted to invite you

~

to their daughter's wedding
to Lord Ponsibly Bigbottom
at All Saints Church, Whitburn

~

It all starts at 4 p.m. on 25 August 2006
then there's dinner and bopping from 6 p.m. till midnight
Dress: very smart
Please bring lots of lovely, big presents
Reply by 1 August, please

P. S. There's a piece of information that Auntie Sarah has written on one invitation that I don't think she should include on the invitation, do you know what it is?

When you receive an invitation

Isn't it great? Don't you feel popular? Won't the invitation look lovely on your mantelpiece or memo board at home?

Angelica has received an invitation to her best friend's birthday party. She is so happy! So excited! She can't wait for Saturday to come. Her friend is having a big party at a theme park, and they've been promised lots of free rides.

But there's one big problem. Angelica hasn't shown the invitation to her parents. She has left it in the bottom of her school bag for the last three weeks. And this Saturday, because her parents didn't know about her invitation, they have booked her in to see the dentist instead.

To avoid this happening to you, once you've admired the invitation and got excited at the thought of the party … *Reply! Reply! Reply!* As soon as you know if you can go. Before you forget.

Immediately show the invitation to your parents or guardian. No matter how grown-up you may think you are, your parents are in control of the family diary and they will have the final say as to whether you can go. They are the ones who know whether Grandma is coming to stay that weekend, what time your brother's football practice is, what time your baby sister needs to be put down for a nap. If you want to go to your friend's party, the sooner you tell your parents about it, the more likely they will be able to juggle things about so that you *can* go.

As soon as you know the answer. Tell your friend at school that you can come (*only* after your parents have okayed it) and then make sure that your parents have replied to your friend's parents. Parents, like children, can be forgetful, so a gentle reminder is not a bad idea.

Sometimes you might not want to reply immediately, just in case a better invitation comes along. Well, I'll be honest with you: I think that's a rotten thing to do! How would you like it if you'd sent out invitations to your party and you heard that some people weren't replying because they were waiting to see if a better invitation was coming their way? I would feel quite hurt and so would you. You have to make a decision and send a reply as soon as possible, and once you've made that decision you have to stick to it.

Put the invitation somewhere you can easily find it. Stick the invitation on your family memo board or wherever invitations usually go. Once you and your parents have replied to it, put a tick on it if you've accepted, or a cross if you've declined. That way you'll know that you remembered to reply.

(P.S. Angelica was lucky. Her parents were able to change her appointment with the dentist to the morning. She did go to the party, and it looks like she's learnt her lesson.)

Before you go...

Have a go at writing and designing your own invitation. It's always worth practising where you're going to put all the information on a dummy copy, before you actually write a 'proper' one that you're going to send out.

Chapter 7

Getting your party started

A note to the grown-ups

I might be in a minority here, but I find hosting my children's parties stressful.

Admittedly, now my children are older (my youngest, Victoria, is fourteen, my eldest, Mark, is twenty-two) their parties have become more manageable, but I still get worried, it's just that the worries have changed. While it used to be: Is he going to share his toys? It's now: Are they drinking alcohol?

I will never forget my first 'nightmare' party.

Mark was going to be four and I felt he was at an age to enjoy having a big party, so I invited about twenty-five of his 'nearest and dearest' to our house. To put you in the picture, we had just moved and totally redecorated – everything was new, shiny and just waiting to be 'appreciated' by a group of hyperactive toddlers. My wife and I had gone overboard in making it look just so – we'd set up a long trellis table laden with home-made beef burgers and sausage rolls, big bowls of green jelly (I'll never forget the colour of the jelly…) and precision-cut finger sand-wiches. It was a mountain of treat foods and orange squash. Balloons floated around the room, party hats and streamers were neatly laid out and twenty-five little chairs were waiting for twenty-five little people to sit on them. My wife and I sighed with contentment when we looked at the pretty picture we had creat-ed and gave ourselves a pat on the back – we had done a good job. Little did we know what was about to happen.

Everything went swimmingly until the children started eating. Suddenly they weren't behaving in the way we wanted them to. They got so excited by the spectacle of the food that they started picking at it all simultaneously. We'd thought that, counting the group of parents who'd said they wanted to stay, we would have enough parental presence to control the situation, but we were wrong. A food fight suddenly erupted. Like a forest fire, it spread from two to four, from four to six children, and their chosen weapon was green jelly. As I came back into the room with the ice cream, my jaw dropped. There was jelly everywhere. Our lovely dining room was a total mess. To give you an idea of how bad it was, the curtains had to be taken down and professionally cleaned, as did the carpet, and the walls had to be washed down and one wall repainted. It took us two days to recover. And the lesson we learnt was invaluable.

The problem was, we'd had unrealistic expectations of the children. We hadn't imagined that any child would throw food around in someone else's house. We hadn't imagined that they'd think that sort of behaviour was acceptable. But then, we hadn't exactly helped the situation. Leaving huge bowls of jelly out on the table was tempting for four-year-olds, not having enough parental supervision meant that any potential bad behaviour wasn't immediately nipped in the bud, and we hadn't considered the effect of putting twenty-five four-year-old children in a room *together*. The line that separates excitement and frenzy is a thin one, especially when it comes to younger children.

Clearly, twelve-year-olds' and six-year-olds' parties are very different: their behaviour and awareness of the world changes by the year. But having unrealistic expectations of our children's behaviour is a problem that can affect us, at any stage of our child's development.

In this chapter we will talk about:

• How to plan a party, so you both have a good time.

• As the host and the 'mini' host, your child's and your responsibilities before, during and after the party.

We put a lot of pressure on ourselves to give our children the best, and birthday parties are one area where we can go totally overboard. Though it might sound trite to say so, a child is going to have a much better time at their party if their parents are relaxed and enjoying the experience, rather than running around like headless chickens, barking orders at each other and rushing out into the garden to numb the pain with a glass of wine or a cigarette.

So while you might want to give your child the most wonderful party, have thirty children in your house, serve them a sit-down tea with home-made biscuits and a beautifully sculptured birthday cake that's taken you two days to perfect, bring in Coco the clown and a funfair as entertainment and make some sophisticated 'nibbles' for the grown-ups, take a deep breath and think … *Hold on! Am I taking on too much?*

To give a good party, you don't need to go mad, and you don't need to exhaust yourself before the party's even started. Food isn't important to children. They don't go away at the end and do an A.A. Gill on your finger sandwiches. What *is* important is having fun. And as you are such an important part of their lives, children not only want you to be there, but they want to see *you* having a good time. That little occasional glance in your direction is to check that everything is right with the world. If they see you stressed, tired and grim-faced, it's not a great birthday present.

There are some adults who effortlessly take stressful situations in their stride. They might be hosting a dinner party, their food might be burnt to cinders; the smoke alarm might be whining in the background, and they will still smile, shrug it off and make a joke of it. There is a great charm in being able to do this. And this charm is born out of an innate confidence – not arrogance – and there's a big difference between the two…

A well-known member of a European royal family was once staying with us. Her son was complaining to a maid about the way his jeans had been pressed and finally, in a temper, he threw them down on to the floor in front of her. In front of the maid, his mother ticked her young son off for having behaved in such an arrogant, thoughtless manner. He clearly took offence and told her she couldn't expect him to sound any other way. He should have the confidence to ask for anything he wanted, after all, one day he was going to be king. His mother said, 'Confident yes, arrogant no. Arrogance is confidence without kindness or humility. Arrogance is a king without a heart.' I was very touched by what she said. I thought it was such an important distinction.

If your children see you deal with stressful situations in an easy-going and confident manner, and, whatever happens, having fun, it'll really help them later on in their lives when they start hosting their own parties and dinner parties, because they won't be fazed by anything, and they'll feel they can handle any situation.

Boundaries

I have seen some truly spectacular children's birthday parties. I remember when the ballroom of a hotel was transformed into a fairground with a merry-go-round, candy-floss machines – all the paraphernalia of a funfair. Real grass had been laid down, and, as the little girl liked rainforests, a rainforest had been imported and recreated in an ante-room. Monkeys and parrots were brought in for the children to play with, and, as a special treat, a rock star and a very famous boy band performed. Presents ranged from Cartier watches to diamonds.

The little girl was seven years old. There were about one

hundred and fifty guests. Did she have fun? Of course she did! Who wouldn't? But she also burst into tears because she was a little in awe of the huge number of guests, and she seemed at her happiest when she was sitting in her father's lap, eating her birthday cake with her mother stroking her hair.

Parties are emotionally charged events, whatever their size (this also goes for tea parties and play-dates with more than three children). Children get incredibly excited, fuelled by the stimulus of other children, sugar, and the thrill of games and presents. All thoughts of considerate behaviour disappear, which is why boundaries of good behaviour are so important and really need to be put in place *before* the event, not during it.

It's important to establish boundaries whatever age your children are. A ten-year-old might fancy the idea of a late-night party that includes loud music, no parents and an 'X'-rated horror film, but that doesn't mean it should happen. Your daughter might want to wear a miniskirt that looks more like a pink pelmet than an article of clothing, but that doesn't mean you should let her. By the way, watch out for 'the friend' that all children seem to bring up in the middle of an argument. 'The friend' whose parents let him or her watch 'anything they want', who bought them an island off the Bahamas for their birthday, who lets them stay up till midnight every night and gave them a sweet shop for Christmas!

Maybe I'm a bit old-fashioned, but as a result of my experiences working with children, I believe that no children of any age *should* be given a free rein. Instead of asking a child 'What would you like?' I believe it's far more healthy to give your child two or three choices that you are happy with, *because your needs as a parent are as important as theirs*. You're the one who has to worry about bills being paid, you're the one who knows how much everything will cost, you're the one who knows what you can manage comfortably so put boundaries in place – say what's possible and what's not before the discussion goes spiralling into the stratosphere and your child starts talking about trapeze artists and hiring a circus tent.

In my experience, children like boundaries. It makes them feel safe. Saying 'No' occasionally and giving a child a *fait accompli* isn't always a bad thing. The secret is to try and do this *before* they enter a highly excitable situation, like a birthday party. Then it's far less likely that things will get out of hand.

I am a great advocate of children being given the chance to talk about their likes and dislikes, and learning to express opinions is a great way for a child to develop, but I also strongly believe there are times when children should simply be told, nicely but firmly, that this is the way things are going to be.

Children are, after all, children. They are not mini-adults. How can a child be expected to choose to eat vegetables over chocolate cake? Why should a child be aware that going to an ice-skating rink is twice as expensive as going to the cinema? Why are we asking children who have only been on this planet for six years whether they're tired and feel like going to bed? Of course they're not going to feel tired. If you ask them, children are never tired! They'll party on until they drop and then be grumpy all the next day.

Children will not always *want* to ask to get down from the table, they can't always be bothered to say 'please', and that's when you, the adult, has to be firm and reaffirm the importance of these boundaries of behaviour: if you don't ask to get down from the table, you *can't* get down from the table; if you don't say please, you *won't* get what you've asked for.

If a child's natural urge is to test boundaries, I really believe it is our responsibility to make sure these boundaries don't wobble or collapse with their first tentative push, like walls in a cheap daytime soap.

It's all in the planning!

Six months before the party

If you're thinking of having the party outside your house, or you're wondering whether to book some entertainment, it's a good idea to start looking into it early. The birthday might seem ages away, but places and people can be booked out up to six months in advance, especially in the summer months.

Once you've done some fact-finding about things they might like to do, present your child with two or three choices that you have already priced up and are happy with. This doesn't mean you and your older child can't sit down and discuss the ingredients of each plan. For example, if they want to buy *that* new football strip and *those* new shoes to wear at their party, they might have to reduce the number of friends they can invite to the cinema. A structure and boundaries will help focus your child's mind.

One month before

Send out the invitations and confirm the venue, entertainers and whatever else you've booked.

Start a list of who's been invited and who has replied, and tick them off as the replies come in.

Casually ask your child for three or four ideas of what

they would like for their birthday so you can hand on the information to aunts and godparents if they ask. I try not to do anything as formal as a list, as I've found it can backfire. Younger children especially might start thinking they're going to get everything on the list.

Two weeks before

Write down the names of children who have dietary medical requirements.

Plan the menu. Decide what food you are going to buy or bake.

For younger children, work out how many parents will be staying on at the party. When I organise children's parties at the Lanesborough for children between the ages of six and eight, I work to an adult-child ratio of four to one. For children between the ages of nine to twelve, a ratio of one to six.

One week before

If you didn't put a 'reply by' date on your invitations, call up the people who haven't yet replied. When you have the total number of guests, put together the party bags and presents.

Decide between yourselves what your child is going to wear, so that it is clean and ready to go on the big day. This ensures there are no tantrums the night before – or, worse, half an hour before.

The day before

Younger children:

Designate a corner of a room as the quiet corner. 'Quiet corners' are very useful. As I've said, parties are emotionally charged events, and for some children it can all become a bit too much. If a child starts to cry, feels sick, or is naughty, a quiet corner is a good place for them to sit down and calm down. Put some books there along with a couple of chairs. After five minutes of 'time out', the child is normally ready to rejoin the fun.

Decide which parts of the house are off limits and show your child. Although you'll be policing the children's whereabouts during the party, it helps if your child doesn't lead a gang of friends into your bedroom and start foraging in your bedside drawers.

Prime your child about his or her responsibilities. Children from six upwards are not too young to be given two or three 'host/hostess responsibilities'. Of course, you'll probably need to gently remind them of those responsibilities during the fun and chaos but, as with toddlers when we lay a knife and a fork for them even before they know how to use cutlery, it's important to get our children accustomed to ways of behaving before we can expect them to copy us automatically.

Put extra toilet tissue in the loo you're going to let the children use. Make sure a clean towel and soap are also within easy reach.

And hide away any breakables so you don't tempt fate.

Older children:

Make a list of rules. Once children are about nine years old, you can start giving them a bit more responsibility. The list of rules gives you the confidence to allow your child the chance to 'host' their own party in the sitting room while you are banished to the kitchen, and gives you the chance to talk through with your child everything that is important to *you* about what should (or shouldn't) happen at the party, thus soothing your nerves.

It might include:

- Areas of the house that are out of bounds

- No swearing

- Having fun, but not making too much noise – maximum volume allowed for music and films

- What to do with the plates and food once they've finished eating. (I leave a rubbish bag out for them to put the wrapping paper, empty pizza boxes and recyclable rubbish in)

- The types of DVD and computer game that are acceptable

- An agreed time when everyone should leave (or go to sleep)

The great thing about a list is that if you have both tacitly agreed to a code of behaviour, you won't have to poke your nose into the sitting room every five minutes and feel like a nag, and the children will appreciate the fact that you are giving them more responsibility and, as a result, respect the rules that you have laid down.

Draw up a seating plan. This might sound formal, but actually it's basic common sense. It's also a good way to encourage your children to get into the habit of considering how they can make their party fun, not just for themselves but for all their guests.

Firstly, if the table's rectangular, it's worth making the point that if they put themselves in the middle of the table, rather than the head, people will be less likely to feel there's a pecking order. Secondly, your child should be aware that if they have boys and girls coming to a sit-down dinner, a seating plan will stop them from following their 'pack' instinct and both sexes herding towards different ends of the table. This also happens when friends come from different schools and parts of your child's life. You don't want anyone to feel excluded – I reiterate this point in my classes. It's so important. And your child will only realise how important a seating plan is if you explain why, or if they're unfortunate enough to be the victim of a poorly thought-out seating plan. Haven't we all been there? Oh dear, the suffering some hosts impose on their guests, and simply because they haven't bothered to consider their personalities and interests.

It takes no more than fifteen minutes to chat your way through a seating plan with your child, but that fifteen minutes can make an important difference between a lively, fun night and a strained, rather indifferent one.

Introductions. The first thing an older child should do when a friend arrives at their house is make sure their guest knows everyone in the room. If they don't, I remind the 'host' that it is their responsibility to make the necessary introductions. You might need to remind your child to do this just before their guests are expected to arrive.

On the day

Younger children:
Prime your child again. Remind them which parts of the house are off limits and what their responsibilities are as the 'host/hostess'.

Designate a present table, ideally somewhere close to the door. Once most of the children have arrived, I transfer the presents upstairs to make way for goodie bags or hats and coats, so that the 'goodbyes' part of the party works as smoothly as the 'hellos'.

Let them help you. Younger children love feeling they are doing something of worth, and directing their energy into something positive, like helping to lay the table, for example, or tying balloons to chairs, works to your advantage. If you don't divert their huge amounts of energy and excitement into something positive, children get so revved up while they're waiting that they can end up jumping around, running through the kitchen, undoing your hard work, and before you know it stressing you out before the party's even started.

Older children:

As all the major issues will have been discussed and agreed on beforehand, you can afford to take more of a back seat. Let them decorate their 'birthday' room – with your help and guidance – and, once you've primed them again on their role as a host/hostess, ticked off the final 'to do' and stuck up the list of rules in the kitchen to remind both of you of what your responsibilities are, all you have to do is retire to the kitchen once everyone has arrived and your presence is no longer required.

Getting your party started

Hosting your own party is one of the most fun things you can do. I don't know about you, but I get excited just thinking about it! What is it that makes parties so much fun? Is it the fact that all your friends are there, being nice to you? Is it the delicious food that your parents have laid out? The fantastic presents your family and friends have given you?

Well, it's everything really. It's the whole shebang!

Now, look again at the above illustration and tell me what you think about Angelica's list of demands.

Angelica gets very excited at least six months before her next birthday. She knows that a good party needs a lot of planning, but *demanding* not *asking* for what you want isn't a great way

135

to talk to anyone, let alone your parents who are trying to help you.

And what's all this about 'no presents, no entry'? Parties are not just about presents. And can you image how sad Harry would be if he wasn't invited to his own sister's party?

The point is, while it is Angelica's party, and it is going to be her big day, the one thing Angelica is forgetting is that the magic ingredient to a party is *fun*. And that doesn't just mean fun for the boy or girl who's hosting the party, we're talking about *everyone* having fun.

When you're hosting your own party you are in a very privileged position. You have the power to make sure everyone is having as good a time as you. You are the centre of attention because all your friends and your family have put you there, so enjoy it! Feeling liked and loved is a wonderful feeling, and you certainly deserve it. But the best parties are the ones where *everyone* has fun (and by the way, that 'everyone' includes your parents and your brothers and sisters as well as your friends – so just because you've had a silly argument with your brother or sister, don't try to hurt them back by not letting them be part of your big day).

Judging by the illustration on page 135, Angelica hasn't quite got the idea yet. By the look on her mother's face she's going to have to rethink her grand plan.

There are quite a few things you can do to make sure you have the best party possible. As you get older, you will naturally be given more responsibility by your parents. But there are plenty of things you can do at any age that will show your parents and your friends how responsible and considerate you are.

Mum and Dad - you can serve the food but then you'll have to go to your bedroom. Robbie and Jen - your job is to take everyone's coats and take away the plates. Harry - if you could stay in the downstairs loo until every -one's left, I'd appreciate it. Now, any questions?

Things to do – younger children

First of all, be patient with your parents! Your mother and father will be working hard to make sure everything is as perfect as it can be. Even if you're having your party somewhere other than your own home, there is still a lot of planning and organisation that your parents have to do. So if your mother and father are rushing around a bit and not immediately answering your questions, or listening to you, understand why.

Now, have a look below at what your responsibilities are as the host or hostess of the party. One thing's for sure – you're a pretty important person! It's in your power to make sure that everyone feels welcome at your party, and it's also in your power to make sure that everyone has as good a time as you. Now that you are six years or over, you have three important duties:

- *Welcome your friends at the door.* When you go to a friend's party, isn't it nice when they open up the door with a smile and a big hello? It makes you feel nice inside, don't you think? It makes you feel welcome. So why don't you do the same?

  If your guests have brought you a present, say thank you and then give the present to your mother or father or put it on your present table. No matter how tempted you are, *do not open any of your presents now!* Save them until after the party. That way, you'll have something to look forward to after all your friends have left.

- *Make everyone feel included in your party.* Remember: there are no best friends at birthday parties. You can't just choose your best friends to play with and ignore all the other children you've invited. How would you feel if you went to someone's party and all they did was talk to and sit next to their 'best' friends? You wouldn't find it a lot of fun, would you? If you do see one of your guests standing alone and looking a bit shy, the really nice thing to do is to go up and talk to them.

- *At the end, say goodbye to your friends and thank them for coming.* All your friends have dressed up and made a real effort to make sure you have a good day, so saying 'goodbye' and 'thank you for coming' are two easy ways of showing you appreciate their efforts. And a 'thank you' to your parents and your siblings isn't a bad idea either.

  When your last friend has left and you're looking forward to opening up your presents, just take a moment to think about all the hard work your mother and father have put into making your day special. The *really* nice thing to do would be to delay opening your presents for ten minutes so you can give your parents a helping hand cleaning up the last few cups and plates.

Top tip!

Write a list of who gave you what present. It will help you when you come to write your thank-you letters.

139

Things you can do – older children

If you're nine or over, you are now at an age where you can be given more responsibility, and I believe it's important that you are. After all, that's the only way you'll learn how to host your own party. However, this doesn't mean that your parents are totally out of the picture, and, to be quite frank, I think it would be a pity if you wanted them to be. Remember, they've got huge amounts of experience when it comes to organising things like parties. Just think how many birthday parties they've had!

When you're planning what to do for your party, try to think about what I call 'cause and effect'. Let's say you want to invite a lot of friends to your party, at least twenty. That will affect where you have your party because of the matter of space. And let's say you'd like to have your party at a very lovely Italian restaurant that your parents have taken you to. That will also affect the number of guests you can invite, because it will definitely cost more than a burger bar. So you have to sit and think, 'What's most important to me? Having lots of friends to my party, or going somewhere special with fewer friends?'

Make a list of rules

Once you've decided what sort of party you're having, a list of rules is a great idea. Your parents and you sit down and discuss what is important to them and what is important to you. For example, if your party is at home, your parents may not want your friends to go into some rooms, or they may ask you not to have the music too loud, and they may give you a time when they would like everyone to leave the house. Now, if you're tempted to start moaning about this, *stop and think!* This is your parents' house as much as it is yours. If you're expecting them to hide in the kitchen or their bedroom, and not keep popping their head round the door every five minutes so you can host your birthday party on your own, there has to be some give and take. Anyway, you all need to sit down and go through the details of the party at some stage.

So writing down a list of rules is a great way of planning your party and reminding each other about what each of your responsibilities are and who's allowed to do what. If your parents are going to trust you with extra responsibility, you must prove to them that you can handle it. And that means not expecting to get everything your own way, and being open to discussion.

Plan a seating arrangement

If your guests are going to be sitting down to eat, it's a good idea to think about who should sit next to whom. For example, if you have two friends who have never met each other, but you know they both love hockey or both support Manchester United, it makes good sense to seat them next to each other.

Top tip!

Seating each of your guests next to someone they have something in common with is a great way to make sure your guests enjoy talking to each other – which will give your party a good buzz!

Other things to think about are:

- If the table's rectangular, put yourself in the middle of the table, rather than the head. That way, you'll have more guests closer to you and your guests will be less likely to feel there's a pecking order.

- If you have boys and girls coming to your party, make sure you mix them up. Seating plans are a great way of making sure that the boys and girls don't end up herding together at different ends of the table.

- Separate best friends. I always say that there should be no 'best friends' at parties, and by that I mean you must try not to show favouritism to any one particular friend. Just think how you would feel if you were invited to a friend's party and all they did was chat to their two best friends the whole evening and ignore everyone else? You wouldn't feel very happy about it, would you? So treat everyone as equals. And if you and your guests have best friends, make sure you separate them all, so no one feels excluded and no one is ignored.

- Write down three things that best describe each friend (for example: good jokes, plays hockey, shy with boys or girls), then see which friends you think would get on well sitting next to each other.

When you've written out your seating plan, write out the names of all your guests on separate slips of paper and, before they arrive, place them on the table in the correct places. That way your guests will know where you would like them to sit. Or, if you like, you can simply read your plan out when all your guests are standing around the table and show each individual guest where to sit. It's up to you how you do it. The most important thing is that you have bothered to think about your guests and their needs.

Remember: it can take about fifteen minutes to chat your

way through a seating plan, but that fifteen minutes can ensure that everyone has a good time.

Make Introductions

On the day, make the effort to introduce people to each other. One thing to be aware of is that when a friend arrives at your party and they don't know everyone standing in the room, they may feel a little shy and a little nervous. One of the ways you can help them relax is by introducing them to people they don't know.

I always think that when you're making an introduction, it's nice to add a brief explanation of how that particular person fits into your life. For example, 'Can I introduce you to Harry? Harry's a friend from my karate classes.' That extra bit of information immediately gives your guests something to talk about.

Why not have a go at introducing each other to an imaginary guest? What would you say about each other?

Say your thank yous!

After the party, all you want to do is open up your presents, but take the time to thank your parents and help them with the tidying up. They will be so grateful, and you will be showing that you can handle the responsibility of hosting your own party.

And when you start on the presents, write a list so you know who to write your thank you letters to.

Before you go...

Now that you've learnt about being a good host or hostess, how would you cope with the following tricky situations? Chat through all the possible answers with your parents or brothers and sisters and see whether you agree with each other. Cover up the answers first.

Who's the host with the most?

Question 1

A friend of yours arrives at your party without a present for you. What do you do?

A. Ask them to go home. You only let friends come to your party if they bring you a present.
B. Don't make a big deal about it. Maybe they forgot? Maybe their parents didn't have time to buy you something? They've made the effort to come to help you celebrate your birthday and that's the most important thing.
C. Ask them why they haven't brought you a present. You deserve an explanation.

I'd say 'B'. Don't put your friend in an embarrassing situation. He or she probably feels bad enough as it is. Remember, as the host or hostess, it's your job to make everyone feel at ease, not give them a hard time.

Question 2

It's your birthday party and you see one of your guests cheating at one of the games. What do you do?

A. Shout out 'CHEAT!' No one should get away with cheating.
B. Stop the game as soon as you see your friend cheating, and make a general, jokey comment like, 'Quite a few of you seem to be keeping your eyes open! Or looking at other people's answers!'
C. If your mother or father is overseeing the game, go over and have a quiet word with them. Let them deal with this so it doesn't get personal.

'B' or 'C'. If your parents are there and they are overseeing the game, it makes sense for them to decide if anything needs to be done. If you're older, and your parents aren't in the room, you can either ignore it, or make a general, jokey comment. Never get personal and embarrass someone – it will not make either you or your friend feel any better.

Question 3
One of your friends doesn't want to join in a game. What do you do?

A. Ask her if she's OK. If she says she is, and she just doesn't want to join in, respect her wishes.
B. Tell her she's being a spoilsport and leave her alone.
C. Tell her she must join in and the game isn't going to start until she does.

Definitely 'A'. You must never draw attention to people because they don't want to join in. Maybe they feel awkward, or shy, or even sick, and they just don't want to make a fuss. If you start making a fuss, all you're doing is making them the centre of attention, but for all the wrong reasons, and they'll just feel really embarrassed. Let them be.

Before you go...

Tell each other three things you have learnt from reading this chapter.

Chapter 8

Partying without your parents

A note to the grown-ups

When your child is with you, it is very easy to police their behaviour. The problem arises when they head off into the big, wide world without you. I don't know about you, but I've had countless nights worrying about the security and the behaviour of my children when they're out at sleepovers, off on a school trip or at a friend's party. In fact, I own up! I'm the dad who's always there to pick up my children bang on time, and very relieved when I find them in one piece, not sporting a pierced tongue or tummy button, not suffering from alcohol poisoning and not doing anything they shouldn't be doing. Oh, what sensational ideas our imaginations concoct! Especially when it comes down to our children's behaviour.

The good news is that, in my experience, our children are never as badly behaved as our imaginations would have us believe. In fact, having talked to parents in my classes, I'd go as far as to say that we don't give our children *enough* credit for listening and taking on board everything we try to teach them. We are not always around when our children are behaving at their very best, but we always seem to be around when our children are behaving at their very worst.

When our children are away from us, it can bring out the best in them. Believe me, I've seen it. They're considerate, they're thoughtful, they listen and converse like real pros. And five minutes before, they could easily have been screaming at their parents, hitting the walls or lying on the floor, being dragged and perfecting their 'limp lettuce' routine.

So try not to worry about the behaviour of your children while they're away from you. The best and most useful thing you can do before your child goes off to a party is to double-check you've ticked off all the boxes that you are responsible for.

Your responsibilities as the adult

Your role is pivotal to the development of your child's social life, and that's a huge responsibility. There are so many things to think about, especially when you're juggling the social lives of more than one child, *and* your own, *and* you and your partner's! I've always thought a carer for a child would give any leading events management company a good run for their money. Planning ahead takes the stress out of the day, which means you and your child arrive at the party feeling relaxed. No one comes to blows having last-minute disagreements, and everyone will be happier for it.

Below are some tips to help things run as smoothly as possible for you.

A week before the party

Double-check the details on the invitation. Is it fancy dress? A sleepover? Swimming? Are they going to be outside? Do they need any specific clothing? Help your child decide what they are going to wear. Obviously older children will want to make their own minds up about what's suitable, so I suggest you let your child try on his or her ideal outfit some time ahead of the party, and then, if it's not suitable, explain why and start again. Sorting out this outfit now means no arguments the night or morning before the party, and it means you won't be wrong-footed the night before when you realise what your child wants to wear is in the wash.

Buying a present

Next time you're in a shop to buy a present and a card, why not buy a few and make a stockpile? This is invaluable in helping you feel in control, and especially handy when your child is in the younger age bracket, when parties seem to follow thick and fast every weekend. Stocking up on wrapping paper, cards and presents means less rushing around for you at the last minute and less stress.

Parents often ask me what a 'polite' amount to spend on a child's birthday present is. From what I gather, about £10 is the going rate. The parents I've chatted to say their biggest bugbears are not cheap toys, but rubbish toys that fall apart at the first touch. For under-tens, educational and fun toys were top of their list.

Leave room for delays

Tell your child you'll be leaving fifteen minutes before the actual time you plan to leave. That will give you and them 'faffing' time. I am a great advocate of faffing time. It allows you and child to talk through a mental checklist. Present? Card? Coat? Swimming trunks? Invitation? Map? Involving your child in the checklist helps them to start taking more responsibility.

Have a contact number

If your child is going to a sleepover, make sure you have a land-line contact number. This ensures that you don't have to depend on your child's mobile. If your child is going to be outdoors, it's good to have the supervising adult's mobile number, just in case you get stuck in traffic or your car breaks down.

Prime your child in the car

A casual chat as you travel to the party is the easiest way to remind them of the basics of good manners at a party. You'll have done all the groundwork at home, so all your child will need is a quick refresher course. Don't make a big thing about it, other-wise your child will start picking up on your stress and they'll react to it. Talking through 'please', 'thank you', 'thank you for having me', and whatever else you'd like to add is probably enough. And then, of course, you can soften the didactic element of your conversation by telling them that the most important thing they *must* do is have fun.

Drop off and pick up on time

This is *really* important. Think of the parents who are hosting the party. They have enough to worry about without fretting 'Is such and such lost? Or are they not coming?' And when it's time to pick up, think how your child will feel if they're the last one left. Little people are sensitive souls, and they'll think you've forgotten about them. Older children suffer the embarrassment of being 'last' in a different way – they feel acutely self-conscious. And the parents giving the party? They're exhausted and want everyone to go home at the time they put on the invitation.

Punctuality is the key to keeping everyone happy. As with all the lessons about good manners in this book, it comes down to consideration and respect for other people.

Top tip!

If you know you are going to be more than fifteen minutes late, pull over and call the parent who is hosting the child's party. If they're waiting outside a swimming pool or theme park it will allow them time to reorganise themselves and make sure that someone will be there to meet you.

In this chapter I will take you and your child through:

- Your child's responsibilities as a guest.

- Escape routes from tricky situations.

Partying without your parents

Isn't it great when you get invited to a party? After you and your parents have replied to the invitation and you've stuck the invitation somewhere safe, all that's left is for you to decide what to wear and look forward to the fun day ahead.

What do you think of the way Harry and Angelica are dressed at the beginning of this chapter? They both look very… well, what can I say? Harry looks like he's about to climb Mount Everest and Angelica looks like she's just stepped off a Hollywood film set. They are having a trying-on session to dress up for Percy's birthday party. Look at the invitation. Are Harry and Angelica correctly dressed?

<u>Invitation</u>

You are invited to
Percy's birthday party!

Please come to: Blackberry Farm
On: October 18th
Time: 12.00 – 3.00 p.m.
Dress: Outdoor clothes

R.S.V.P. by 14 October Frances
0191 777 8888 or
Frances@gardenhouse.com
Map is attached!

Well, I suppose Harry's clothes *are* outdoor, but they're really meant for skiing. And Angelica is dying to wear her dress, she loves it so much, but it's not exactly a good idea to wear it to a farm.

Now, what do you think about the way Robbie and Jen are dressed?

Doesn't Robbie look smart? He's wearing a jacket and tie, which means he must be going somewhere quite special. Jen, on the other hand, is wearing jeans and trainers, so she looks quite relaxed. But do you know what? They're both going to the same party. Do you think they are both dressed correctly? Have a look at Jen's invitation and see what you think.

Invitation

You are invited to attend a birthday tea for
Davinia Bigbottom

at Hugehouse Manor
on 12 October at 4.00 p.m. – 6.00 p.m.
Dress: jacket and tie

R.S.V.P. by 30 September
Sarah 0208 020 8020 or
Sarah@hugehouse.com

It says 'jacket and tie', so it looks like Robbie's OK. What about Jen? Obviously she's not expected to wear a jacket and tie because she's a girl, but does that make it OK for her to wear jeans?

I'll let you in on a secret – Jen has deliberately not bothered to dress up. Davinia is Auntie Sarah's new step-daughter, and to be quite honest Jen thinks she's a bit annoying, so she really can't be bothered to make the effort. But she does want to go to the party because she's heard that a pop star might be there. The question is, do you think Jen is behaving in a considerate way towards Davinia and Auntie Sarah?

Sometimes we may not feel like making an effort, but what we must always remember is that other people's feelings – not just our own – are affected by how we act.

If you accept an invitation, read the invitation and check how your host or hostess is advising you to dress. Otherwise, like Angelica and Harry, you could feel uncomfortable or ruin your favourite clothes. And if, as in Jen's case, you accept an invitation half-heartedly, well, that's not a nice way to approach a party, is it? The good news is that Jen realised she was acting a little thoughtlessly and she's decided to go up to her room and change, and she's promised herself to make an effort with Davinia.

The fact is, there are lots of different types of parties. That's why invitations are so important – they tell us what type of party our friend is planning: a sleepover, football or cinema party. As the guest, you're in a very lucky position. You don't have to think about buying food, tidying the house to make room for more people, or organising entertainment. You and your parents have only three responsibilities. Have a look at the list below and pick out the three that you think are the right ones.

1. To serve the food at the party
2. To reply to the invitation as soon as possible
3. To win all the games
4. To turn up to the party on time
5. To dress appropriately
6. To eat as much as possible

The answers are 2, 4 and 5. One extra thing to add to the list – it's also nice to turn up with a present and a card!

Once you're at the party, there are three things you could do that I think are very important. Your parents can't do these things for you because they're not at the party, so this is a time when you can show how thoughtful and grown-up you are.

Which of the following would you choose?

1. To say please if you're asking for something
2. To make as much noise as possible
3. To be respectful of someone else's house
4. To thank your friend's parents for inviting you
5. To start a food fight

Do I need to say that 1, 3 and 4 are definitely my top three?

It's really pretty easy being a guest – after all, you're meant to enjoy yourself. But it's just as important to help your friend celebrate his or her birthday in the best and most happy environment. Now, that's not a bad job either, is it? However, you can sometimes find yourself in a tricky situation, so below are a few of the questions I'm most often asked by children in my classes.

Escape routes from tricky situations

If you don't like some of the food you've been given. Have a look at page 98 in Chapter 5. This is all about sharing a meal with other people. Move the food you don't like to one side of your plate and leave it. Don't make a fuss. There's no need to.

If someone asks you to dance. What's wrong with that? I'd feel flattered! If you're a bit shy or you don't know the boy or girl, try not to do the automatic thing which is to go bright red, giggle and mumble 'no'. Remember, the boy or girl who has asked you to dance has been very brave to stand up, walk towards you and ask you, so why not say, with a smile on your face, 'Yes!' You'll be making them a happy person, and you never know, you may end up actually having a good time. After you dance together, thank the boy or girl and rejoin your friends.

If you feel sick. Tell a grown-up immediately. They will look after you and if necessary call your parents. You certainly will not be seen as making a fuss.

If someone isn't very nice to you. They're being a bit silly, aren't they? Try to avoid them, and if they continue to be annoying, tell a grown-up. Children like that need to be sorted out by a grown-up, not a child.

If you see someone cheating at a game. Well, this isn't your party, you're a guest, so I'd suggest not making a fuss and drawing attention to the person. Shouting out 'Cheat!' doesn't really add to the 'feel-good' feeling of your friend's birthday party, does it? Just think about this – if you've noticed someone cheating, then you can bet your bottom dollar that other people will have noticed as well. So leave it to the host or hostess's parents to deal with, if they decide to.

If there's a seating plan, and you see you're seated next to someone you don't know. Whatever you do, *don't* swap your name with someone else's. This is the worst thing you can do. Your friend has sat you there for a reason. They have spent time thinking about who you would enjoy sitting next to. So, as you are their guest, *respect their wishes.* If you feel shy, why not start off a conversation with one of the people sitting next to you by asking them some questions about themselves? They're probably feeling as shy as you and will appreciate your attention.

Thank you, please come again!

The party's over, your parents have picked you up, and you're back home with your goody-bag, relaxing. What a great party! Didn't you have a great time? Wasn't the food delicious? Didn't your friend's mother look great dressed up as Mrs Incredible?

Wouldn't it be nice to tell your friend and her parents how much you enjoyed the party?

Thank-you letters are such lovely things. Just think, if you and your parents had spent a lot of time running around organising your birthday party, buying the right food and clearing the house to make way for all your friends, wouldn't you like it if your friends bothered to send you (and, most importantly, your parents) a little note to thank you, saying what a good time they had?

And that's all it needs to be. A little note. You don't need to send a huge letter. Have a look at the note that Angelica and Harry have sent Percy's parents.

Dear Mr and Mrs Hooper and Percy,
Thank you so much for inviting us to Percy's birthday party. We had a great time! Harry loved the birthday cake that you made for Percy, and I thought the magician was really very good.
Love
Angelica and Harry

A thank-you letter doesn't take much time to write, but it gives the person who receives it a *lot* of pleasure. It makes them feel that all their hard work has been appreciated. And that's a good thing, wouldn't you agree?

Top tip!

When you're writing a thank-you letter, always try to mention one thing about the party that you really enjoyed. For example, Harry mentioned the birthday cake, while Angelica mentioned the magician. This makes your thank-you letter a little bit more special.

Before you go...

Why not try writing each other a thank-you letter for something you have recently done for each other?

Tell each other three things that you have learnt from reading this chapter.

Chapter 9

The good things in life

A note to the grown-ups

Good manners – or the lack of them – are one of the biggest causes of arguments in modern life. For parents, manners are often the reason for *another* exhaustive argument with their child. How often have you heard yourself, with a heavy heart, launch yet another directive: 'Now I told you, Johnny, *don't* sit like that, and for goodness' sake, wipe your mouth with your napkin, *not* your hand!' Johnny makes a face and, in turn, with an equally heavy heart, wonders what all the fuss is about.

And so it goes on, the rebuke and the rebellion. Both adult and child stuck in a vicious circle, wondering why on earth life seems so difficult.

Children can perceive manners as boring. Adults can see them as a good reason to get irritated with people.

'So I opened the door for her, and she didn't even say thank you! How rude!'

'It's my right of way, but I let him go anyway, and he didn't even wave! What an ungrateful man!'

'Why didn't they at least call to tell me they were going to be late? They're so inconsiderate!'

If good manners are such a positive thing, why do they create so much angst?

One of my main intentions in writing this book has been to change your children's, and hopefully your own, perception of what good manners can mean. They don't have to mean arguments, nagging, losing your temper or pulling-your-hair-out frustration. They can be about puzzles, games and learning together. Suddenly, both of you see that good manners can be good fun, and with that, the grey cloud of stress is lifted. It's been great seeing children and parents visibly relax when they realise this.

The more research I do with children, the more I realise it's the *presentation* of an idea, not the idea itself, that dictates its success or failure. So bear this in mind when you're going through things with your own child. See the fun in learning and so will they.

In my view, good manners belong with the good things in life (beach holidays, a good bottle of wine and a romantic weekend away with my wife) because, to me, good manners are anything but dreary or boring. They are inspiring and uplifting. And *life-changing*. Does that sound trite? A trifle sensationalist? I don't think so.

I've seen the look on a maid's face when two children have summoned her to their suite for the twentieth time in an hour. And why did they call her? Not to ask for anything, but simply to time her and see how quickly she responded to their bell. It was a brother and sister team who did this, and the worst thing about this story for me is that their parents knew what their children were doing but did nothing to stop them. The maid was a lovely Irish girl with great spirit, but you should have seen her after the children had finished with her. She looked angry and humiliated and hurt to the core. The lack of respect these children had shown her had deeply upset her. And in return, her upset affected the people around her.

And let me tell you about the most wonderful Hollywood film star who has stayed a number of times at the hotel with his family. He is incredibly charming, and it's plain to see that his charm and respect for other people has rubbed off on to his children. They are a pleasure to be with, and because of this, everybody wants to help them and there is always a good feeling whenever you are in their company.

Manners, or a lack of them, can change the feel of a situation, immediately. A sudden smile, an 'excuse me' or the simple act of turning off a ringing mobile can defuse a possibly negative situation.

In this chapter, we talk through the many small things children can do on a day-to-day basis to encourage good feeling in life, not just for themselves, but also for the people around them. As is the case with all the chapters, your child will need *your* help to recall and put into practice the individual lessons. There's no CD ROM we can play to them while they're asleep. Unfortunately, life's not that easy.

But then again, on reflection, I'm not very sure if I'd want it to be. When I look back at all the little battles and conquests my wife and I have been through – getting Mark to use his knife, persuading Peter to say please and thank you, pleading with Victoria to tidy her room, refusing to let Joseph stay out late, and finally succeeding in getting Allana to let other people get a word in edgeways – in a funny way, I miss it all.

OK, sometimes it's been tough. And in my professional life I've occasionally despaired that some of the children I've taught would *ever* realise the importance of respect and consideration for other people. I've feared they would turn into adults who would never realise the value of other people's needs and feelings. But these are the same children who now, as young adults, are respectful and charming, and who I am truly honoured to know.

Looking back, I know the greatest times for me have been when I've seen my wife's and my hard work rewarded.

I hope that by now you have experienced that wonderful feeling when your child does something that makes you so proud your heart wants to sing. Trust me, you have many of those times ahead, so please don't be tempted to give up reminding your children about everything we've talked about. It might feel like a slog, and sometimes you'll wonder if you can be bothered to go on, but believe me when I say – now I look at my own 'adult' children – I know it is all worth it.

Mad as it may sound, *enjoy it!* Enjoy every funny, irritating, frustrating, uplifting, maddening bit of your and your children's life together. Because, like all the most precious things in life, they'll be gone before you know it.

The good things in life

What do you consider to be the good things in your life? Chocolate ice cream? Presents? Summer holidays? These are the obvious things, things you think of straight away. But then there are other things that are not as obvious, but just as, if not more, important.

Imagine you're having lunch with a friend, and their mobile goes off. Your friend answers the call and then starts having a conversation that goes on … and on … and on. And you're left at the table, eating your food, with no one to talk to. How would that make you feel?

Or let's say the same friend comes to your house for tea and goes to use your loo. And then, when you go to use the loo, the loo seat is up and there are drips of wee around the loo seat. *Yuck!* How horrible is that? What would you think about your friend?

In both cases, I'd think, 'It's time they started thinking about other people as much as themselves!'

The good things in life are the little things we can do on a daily basis to make other people happy. Things like *not* chatting on your mobile when you're sitting with your friend and *always* making sure you leave the loo seat the way you found it! These are the little considerate things that, separately, may not seem important, but all together can make a big difference.

You might ask, what's the point in trying to make other people happy? After all, are *you* going to benefit from doing something nice for someone else? But tell me, are you going to feel happier if you're nice to someone, or happier if you don't bother?

Let's say you're going into a shop and you see an old lady

with a walking stick coming towards you. You're standing at the door. What do you think you should do?

A. Ignore her.
B. Hold the door open for her and say, 'After you'.
C. Walk quickly through the door so you don't have to deal with her.

Well, of course you could ignore her, you could walk quickly through the door, but if you do 'B', the lady will give you a great big smile, she'll say 'thank you', and she'll be very grateful to

you for being so kind and thoughtful to her. And then something quite amazing will happen to you – you will find yourself smiling and you will feel on top of the world.

Top tip!

Something happens to all of us when we do something nice for other people. It's a feeling that's as comforting as a milky cup of chocolate when you're cold, or a hot bath filled with bubbles when you're tired. It starts in your heart and warms you up from the inside out. I call this feeling an 'angel hug', and you only get this feeling when you do good things for other people.

There are a few things you can do in everyday life to show you care about other people and their feelings:

Respect older people... When people get older, sometimes they find it more difficult to do things – simple things like walking, or hearing, or seeing. Imagine how you would feel if you suddenly couldn't hear what your best friend was saying to you? Or if you found you couldn't run any more? One thing's for sure, you wouldn't like it if people laughed at you. And you wouldn't like it if people became impatient with you. So next time you come into contact with older people, remember, you may need to be patient.

...and younger children. Younger boys and girls will always look up to you, simply because you're older. They'll think you're pretty cool, and that means they'll try to copy everything you're doing. So if you're in the company of younger children, think: Are they safe trying to do all the things I'm doing, and do I need to look after them?

Hold the door open for other people. It's such a simple thing to do! It takes no extra effort and people love it. If someone is carrying a lot of bags, or pushing a pushchair, or someone's in a wheelchair, holding the door open for them can really make life easier for them.

Be considerate with your mobile phone. If you have one, you'll know how useful they are. If your friends have one, you'll also know how noisy they can be. Funny things happen to people's voices when they start speaking into mobile phones: they raise their voices and they start shouting into their phone as if their friend was living at the North Pole. If you have a mobile, before you pick up a call, *think*! If you're sitting with someone having lunch, do you have to take the call? Wouldn't it be better to let it go to your messages and then call the caller back later? That way, the friend you're having lunch with won't feel ignored, and you won't feel stressed trying to turn a ten-minute phone conversation into a one-minute one.

I get very cross when I see two people sitting having lunch together, and one of them spends most of lunch answering their phone. Why? Because they're not thinking about their lunch companion's feelings. After all, how would they like it if the tables were turned and they were the ones sitting there, feeling ignored?

Top tip!

If you're with a friend or a grown-up and your phone rings and it's important that you take the call, say 'Excuse me', go to a quiet place, and be as quick as you can.

Even better, if you're expecting a call, but you're with friends, put your mobile on to vibrate. That way, it won't disturb anyone.

Keep your voice down. Have you ever been in the cinema or at the theatre and something major has happened – a really important part of the film or play has just unfolded – and instead of hearing it, you just hear the people sitting next to you chattering on about their favourite football team? Why are these people here? I always wonder. Don't they want to watch the film? The truth is that when you go to the cinema with friends, you are bound to want to make the occasional comment or joke, but the secret is to do it quietly. When you're in public places like libraries, cinemas, theatres and museums, respect the fact that you're sharing the space with other people, and that while your friend might want to hear everything you say, the rest of the public doesn't. This rule also applies to continuously rummaging your hand around your bag of popcorn, slurping on fizzy drinks and generally being a noisy eater.

Be tidy going to the loo. Well, it's basic common sense but, if you're a boy, *always* put the loo seat down after you've finished. And always leave the loo as you found it – that means boys *and* girls! Leave the loo roll where it should be (not rolling around on the floor), the towel hanging up and the soap in the soap dish. By the way, if you're at someone else's house or in a public place, before you do anything, always check there's some toilet tissue in the loo. And if you use the last piece, tell a grown-up so they can replace it.

Introduce your friends to your parents. When you've got new friends coming round to your house, or your parents are picking you up from a school activity and you're chatting to some friends they don't know, why not introduce them? It takes a couple of minutes and it means you're sharing part of your life with your parents, something your parents will really appreciate.

Say hello to your friends' parents. You go round to their house, raid their fridge, hog their television and then you 'hang out', finally leaving them at the end of the day with an atomic mess of empty glasses, toys and plates to tidy up. Well, maybe you don't do all of the above (in fact, I'm sure you always make an effort to tidy up when you leave a friend's house!) but I just want to make the point that a 'Hello, Mr and Mrs Johnson, how are you?' and a 'Bye, Mr and Mrs Johnson, thanks for having me' are two great ways of beginning and ending your visit. If you've never met a friend's parents before, shaking hands with them, smiling and saying something like 'Hello, nice to meet you' is a good opener.

Keep your room tidy. Well, let's be honest, there's no reason why your parents should tidy your mess up for you, is there?

Look at it this way. Do you have opinions? Would you like your parents to listen to you? Do you like the idea of your parents seeing you as a person who is responsible and can be trusted with certain things, like turning the TV on when you like to watch your favourite programmes, or going out on your own to play football with your friends, or being allowed to have your friends round for tea and not have your parents in the room with you?

If you think you are old enough to do any of those things, don't you think the least you can do is keep your room tidy?

It doesn't take much effort. And believe me, it's a great way of showing your parents that you deserve the chance to be given greater freedom when it comes to other parts of your life.

Because keeping your clothes and your possessions tidy and ordered in your bedroom and around the house shows that you're thinking about other people *and* that you are grown-up enough to take responsibility for your own things.

Half the problem with bedrooms is when you don't have enough storage space to put things away. If this is the case, label shoeboxes or ask your parents for some plastic storage boxes so you can put away your clothes and your toys/possessions. Labelling the boxes means you'll always know which box to tidy your stuff away into, as well as being able to find your things quickly and easily when you need to.

Messy rooms happen when you let piles of 'things' grow. One day it will be a sock, the next day a sock, 2 CD covers and a jumper, the day after an empty packet of crisps, three socks (non-matching), two T-shirts, a school exercise book, and before you know it … this will happen:

So, I suggest that, at the end of every day, perhaps just before your tea, or before you get into bed, you take five minutes out to tidy up your room. Just five minutes! You'll be amazed how much you can do, and if you do it every night, you'll never get to the stage where, like Robbie, you can't even see your own bed. And you'll always be able to find your favourite clothes and possessions when you need to.

Help your parents around the house. A little effort goes a long way. Why don't you offer to help by laying the table or clearing the plates at the end of a meal? Or if you see that the post has arrived and is strewn all over the floor, why not pick it up? These are such small things, but as we've discussed they can really make a big difference to the way that your parents see you and appreciate you.

Experiment

Why don't you pick one good thing to do from the above list and try to remember to do it everyday this week? Ask yourself at the end of the week how you feel.

One final thought for you:

The greatest gift we all have is the ability to make each other happier people. And that's what good manners are all about. It's simple really, isn't it?

Recipes

Sticky Glazed Chicken Drumsticks

Serves six

Ingredients

Six chicken drumsticks

For the marinade

2 tbsp dark soy sauce

1 clove of garlic, crushed

1 tsp five-spice powder

1 tsp ground peppercorns

$^1/_2$ tsp ginger

2 tsp honey

Method

1. Mix all the marinade ingredients together.
2. Place the drumsticks in a polythene bag, pour in the marinade and rub to cover. Seal and leave to chill overnight.
3. Turn on to a baking tray and cook in a preheated oven, 180°C/350°F or Gas Mark 4, for 30-40 minutes until brown.

Chow Mein

Ingredients

125g (4oz) Chinese egg noodles

2 tbsp sesame oil

3 tbsp groundnut oil

4 spring onions, sliced

1 clove of garlic, crushed

2 carrots, cut into sticks 7.5cm (3in)

25g (1oz) cucumber, cut into sticks

125g (4oz) thin green beans, halved

125g (4oz) shiitake mushrooms, thickly sliced

300ml ($^1/_2$ pint) chicken stock

2 tbsp Chinese oyster sauce

1 tbsp cornflour

2 beaten eggs

Salt, pepper, sugar to taste

Method

Cook the noodles according to the package instructions, drain them and toss them in the sesame oil. Set aside.

Heat 2 tablespoons of the groundnut oil in the wok, add the spring onions, garlic, carrots, cucumber and beans and stir-fry for two minutes. Add the shiitake mushrooms and stir-fry for one minute.

Add the chicken stock, salt, pepper, and a pinch of sugar, then cover and simmer of two minutes.

Blend the Chinese oyster sauce and cornflour with a little water, stir into the vegetables and bring the mix to a good simmer. Toss in the noodles and transfer to a warmed dish.

Heat the remaining oil in a small frying pan and make a flat top soft omelette with the eggs, lightly scrambling it. Stir into the chow mein and serve immediately.

Fruit on a snow mountain

Bite-size pieces of fruit on ice to be picked at with chopsticks.

Ingredients
1 ripe mango
1 small pineapple, peeled and cut into chunks
2 kiwi fruits, peeled and cut into chunks
2 pears, cored and cut into chunks
250g (8oz) lychees, peeled (or 425g [15oz] can, drained)
250g (8oz) strawberries

Method
1. Cut the mango each side of the stone, then peel and cut it into chunks.
2. Toss the fruit in a little orange juice.
3. Put all the chunks of fruit on crushed ice.
4. Decorate the base with flowers, and serve with ice cream.

Responses to
Manners from Heaven

Joanne Admiraal, mother of Christabel (2), Stanley (3), Claudia (11) and George (12), London:
'It's a fabulous way to teach your children all about good manners while brushing up on your own at the same time!'

Claudia: 'It's really interesting. I didn't know that was why you're supposed to eat your soup that way, but it actually makes sense.'

Pippa and George Miller, parents of
Johnny (7) and Hal (9), London.

George about Hal: 'What a result! Hal
and I didn't come to blows when we were
reading it and, I'll be honest, I think I
found going through the chapters with
Hal as informative as Hal did.'

Pippa about Johnny: 'We've had fun
reading the chapters together and the
best thing is, Johnny actually remembers
what we've talked about.'

Johnny: 'I liked the games. Mixing the
cutlery up was my favourite bit.'

Julie Grant, mother of Beckie (12) and Elinor (8), Cleadon, Sunderland:
'As a primary school teacher and mother I found the book really useful. It goes into the sort of practical detail you need, but Elinor loved the games and the puzzles so much, it never felt like hard work.'

Elinor: 'I loved learning how to use chopsticks. Mummy and I had a Chinese banquet to practise using them, which was a lot of fun.'